THE
INSIDERS
GUIDE
TO A

Praise for
The Insiders Guide to a Free Ride

Mr. Burns has provided a great method, actually a set of tools, for building your scholarship application, and developing a support team to help you reach your higher education goals.

–Thomas C. Keane, Director of Financial Aid for Cornell University

As someone who applied for 72 scholarships in a year, Marvis knows what he is talking about. He approaches the question of 'Is college worth it?' from a financial, social, and professional perspective rather than simply telling students they should go because it is good for them. The reasons for going to college have changed and through this book, Marvis teaches students how to play the new game in order to graduate debt-free, highly connected, and fully employed.

–Jullien Gordon, Motivational Speaker Stanford GSB Graduate

The Insiders Guide to a Free Ride

Marvis Burns

EDUCATIONAL KEYS Publishing ©

NEW YORK, NY

Insiders Guide to a Free Ride

Published by Educational Keys, Inc.

Copyright © 2012 by Marvis Burns
ISBN-13: 978-0-985-57240-2
ISBN-10: 0-985-57240-X

Layout and Cover Design by Educational Keys, Inc.
Edited by Penelope Love and Educational Keys, Inc.

www.educationalkeys.com
www.marvisburns.com
Direct all inquires to: book@educationalkeys.com

Manufactured in the United States of America

EDUCATIONALKEYS

UNLOCKING GREAT MINDS

WWW.EDUCATIONALKEYS.COM

To all of my family, friends, and supporters, who collectively made this book possible.

Contents

PREFACE

These days, the scariest thing about applying to college isn't sitting by the mailbox, waiting to find out if you've been accepted to the school of your dreams.

It's wondering how you can possibly afford the school of your dreams. Or, for that matter, any school at all.

If college has been on your mind, whether you've been planning for it since you were in pre-school or only recently started thinking that it might be the right next step for you, chances are you've heard a few financial horror stories. Maybe you've seen the articles about young adults entering the workforce saddled with tens of thousands – and even hundreds of thousands – of dollars in student loan debt. Maybe you've heard the so-called "experts" and pundits (most of whom, ironically, have college degrees) pose the until-now-unheard-of question, "Is College really Worth the Cost?"

I'll say right now and unequivocally, it is.

However, there's still a very good and very real reason for all this higher-education hysteria. The cost of a college education is skyrocketing, with tuition and fees at both public and private institutions rising six-fold since the early '80s. That's more than double the rate of inflation. The consumer price index has only increased two-and-a-half times in the same period. The result? The cost of a college education is prohibitively expensive for a surprisingly large number of students.

Specifically, I'm talking about students who fall outside of two income silos: those whose familes have the money to handle these increased tuition fees, or those whose parents' total income is below the national poverty line and are most likely to receive government help. If you're one of those people in the middle – and many bright and talented high school students are – you may feel like you shouldn't even be thinking about college at all, simply because you're afraid you can't afford it.

Well, I have good news for you. All that college-is-impossible-so-don't-even-think-about-it stuff is a myth. An urban legend. It is so flat out, totally and completely WRONG that I've written an entire book just to prove it.

•   •   •

The fact is, anyone who crafts a powerful application that "ticks the right boxes" can earn a college scholarship – whether your parents can handle the full cost of tuition, are classified as "low-income," or fall into that middle area. This book explains, in plain English and easy to follow steps, exactly how you can craft the most competitive application possible to take advantage of the vast scholarship opportunities that are available to you.

If you want and deserve the best quality education this country has to offer, but don't have the money to pay for it, I'm here to tell you that you do have options. A few years ago, I was right where you are now. I was motivated to improve my quality of life through higher education. I was smart enough to do the work. I was focused enough to earn the degree.

And I was energetic enough to do whatever it took to increase my chances of ultimate success.

If that sounds like you, you've come to the right place – even if you don't see yourself as the "scholarship type" yet. The bottom line is, it absolutely doesn't matter who you are or where you come from. With costs as high as they are, with the economy weakened and the middle class shrinking, all kinds of people are discovering they need help paying for higher education. You may be the first person in your family to pursue a college degree, or a foreign student who hopes to join the legions of kids who come to the U.S. to take advantage of what is – at least at this writing – still the best college education system in the world. Or you might be from a typical middle-class background with college-educated parents who have been "priced out" of the market for an elite private school, or even a state school.

Wherever you fit in, whatever your college dreams may be, there is more aid available to help you attain your aspirations than you might think.

Each year, thousands of local, state and national organizations collectively allocate more than a billion dollars to scholarships. And believe it or not, every year, millions of those dollars go unclaimed...for the simple reason that a lot of high school students have no idea that that their grades, athletic abilities, and/or extracurricular activities can help them win those scholarship dollars.

Of course you know scholarships exist. I'm sure you know that if you're student body president, captain of the football team and have a 4.0 (unweighted) GPA, you're probably going to be given a big ol' pile of cash to help you attend the school of your dreams.

•   •   •

What you might not know, however, is that you don't have to be Mr. or Miss Spectacular to earn college scholarships. You just have to know where to look, and what to do once you find them. And for most students, that means learning to tell the "story" of who you are and what makes your future a good investment.

Is it easy? Not by a long shot. The application process for these scholarships is rigorous and requires solid preparation, consistent attention and a whole lot of patience, as well as a positive attitude and persistence on your part.

Which, ironically, are the same things you'll need to do well in college anyway. What I can share with you are my own experiences. I've been there, I've done the research, and I know firsthand some of the best kept secrets that will put you ahead of the crowd when you apply for scholarships. This information has been collected from a wide range of experts, including admission counselors, national scholarship committee members, scholarship winners and other people with real, inside knowledge of the higher education field.

•   •   •

Whether you're a freshmen just starting to think about scholarships or a senior with only a few months to go, this book will not only help you discover where to find scholarships that are best for you, but help you craft an application that will get you noticed. You will learn to write better essays, improve your letters of recommendation, sell yourself in interviews, and master several other strategies that will make sure you stand out from other applicants. These are proven strategies that countless students have used not only to land scholarships, but to increase the amount of scholarship dollars won.

This book will also help you develop a solid organizational strategy that will keep you on track as you apply for multiple scholarships, even those with immediate deadlines. In essence, this is a book about details – because it's the details that make the difference between a good application and a winning application.

Again, I want to stress that winning scholarships is not easy. Scholarships are competitive, and the simple act of applying for one alone is not going to win you any cash – especially when some scholarships have 100 or more applicants for each available award. This book is about building an application that will put you ahead of those other hundred applicants.

In other words, what you're holding in your hand is the insider's guide to a free ride. Apply the guidelines I've laid out here, and you will create a scholarship application that sets you apart from your competition and sells the unique, gifted and special investment that is you.

So let's get started – we have a lot of work to do.

Section 1 – The Preparation

The Vegetarian Resource Group offers two $5,000 scholarships per year to students who can prove that they are practicing vegetarians or vegans, and have promoted their lifestyle and beliefs at school and/or in their community. Winning students are required to provide documentation of their vegetarianism and their efforts to promote world peace by not eating meat.

Getting Started

"What does it take to win a scholarship?"

If you've just started thinking about the realities of how you're going to pay for your college education, chances are that question is probably on your mind. Or, maybe more specifically, "Do I, personally, have what it takes to win a BIG scholarship?"

You might wonder if, to win a scholarship, you need to be one of those practically superhuman types, like our hypothetical Straight A-Class-President-Football-Team-Captain – we'll call him Mr. Spectacular. Or are there actually scholarships available for people like you, a mere mortal with actual, human flaws?

Lucky for you (and for 99% of the students out there), the latter is true. If you have the grades, ambition and record of achievements that enable you to consider a college education in the first place, chances are you have the raw materials you need to craft a winning scholarship application.

But notice that phrase..."craft a winning scholarship application." Right away, that implies work, and even creativity, on your part. Your concept of scholarships may be limited to the type of scholarships that are awarded like prizes – where all of a sudden, some club or organization or college starts showering Mr. Spectacular with money and gifts, as if he were Miss America...or maybe Mr. America.

And yes, this does happen. It may even happen to you, if you've performed at an especially high level during your high school career.

However, in most situations, getting a scholarship is more like filling out a college application, or even a job application. You'll fill out a form. You may be asked to write an essay, or perform some other kind of task. In other words, you will have a personal opportunity to communicate with the scholarship organization and share information about you – and in the process, hopefully...

- Provide an application that showcases your uniqueness, talents and accomplishments

- Tell a captivating story that resonates well with the committee

- Distinguish your application from your peers

- Show them exactly why You and Your Future are more worthy of their investment than some other candidate's future.

Telling Your "Story"

Why should an organization select *you*, and not someone who applied right before or after you? It has everything to do with your story. And laying the groundwork for that story – creating a future worth talking about and investing in – starts now. Of course, if you're reading this book and are that serious about your education, chances are you've already started.

If you haven't, understand that no matter what grade you're in, there are things you can be doing *right now* to build your "story" and develop yourself into the student these organizations will be fighting to give money to. It really is never too late, as long as you're willing to do the work.

Who are these magical, scholarship-giving entities you want to appeal to? They're non-profit organizations, corporations, churches, agencies, even individuals...just about anyone that has appreciation for education and money to give to support it. You can find them on websites like scholarships.com, through your high school guidance counselor, in and around your community, and also on my website.

What scholarships all have in common is that they give an entity with money an opportunity to invest that money in You and Your Future. And in order to invest that money in the Business of You in the first place, as opposed to the Business of Someone Else, there's an expectation that the organization will derive something from that investment.

I'm not talking about anything as specific as promising to work for the organization, or even in the field the organization is based in (although you certainly can if you want to). All that matters, in most cases, is that you reflect and/or embody the values and mission the organization thinks are important.

So you might not need to be a straight-A student, or a varsity athlete, or a highly involved student leader – but at the same time, every one of those things, and everything that you are that doesn't involve watching TV, texting your friends, surfing the web or listening to music – helps build your story. Every passion, every interest, every honor and every accolade helps, because every element is a part of what makes you uniquely you. And that's what scholarship committees ultimately want – to invest in a unique *individual* they feel great about, who they feel is the perfect example of who they are and what they stand for.

Because of this, the best part of the whole "story" concept is that it gives you "wiggle room." That's the opportunity that comes with every story, where you can take what might otherwise be your flaws, or weaker points in your story, and explain them in a way that makes them a part of the overall picture, actually strengthening your uniqueness and personal identity.

You get to explain *why* you're not perfect, and show the "deciders" exactly how the choices you made and the things you did with your time prove that you are the most deserving candidate for their money.

For example:

> *"My grades aren't stellar, but I still managed a challenging course load while spearheading a charitable organization,"*

...and,

> *"I didn't have a lot of time for extracurricular activities because I had to work to help support my family, but I got straight A's and made the honor roll for eight straight semesters"*

...are really great stories.

Not that your story has to be either of those things. What makes a great story is that it's uniquely you – and not something that applies to every Mr. Spectacular at every high school in America. It's all about what makes you unique, an individual person with interests and passions and something to offer. And if you are able to show you've had all different kinds of experiences, with a common thread of excellence or passion or commitment running through them, you just might leave poor Mr. S. in the dust.

We'll talk more in detail about telling your story a few chapters down the line, but for now, here are a few questions you can ask yourself that might spark ideas for an overall "theme" that you can develop into a full-*fledged story.*

- What are you passionate about...and why? What excits you? What keeps you up at night?

- Have you ever experienced adversity – and if so, what has it taught you?

- If you were a stock, what would your yield be – and how do you know?

What all of this means is, if you haven't already, now is the time to get serious. From now on, you need to remember the decisions you make, the opportunities you seek, the way you spend your time – it all enhances your story. So at this point in the process, your goal is to fill your "chapters" with as many great "story points" as possible. For example:

- If your story is about your passions, what are you doing to pursue those passions?

- If your story is about adversity, how are you working to overcome it?

- If your story is about your value as a "stock," what are you doing to "add value"?

In other words, your story is about you taking action – which means, if you're spending the bulk of your free time on Facebook or watching "Real World" reruns, it's time to get out there and start doing the kinds of things that will get you noticed. Or at least give you something to talk about other than celebrity gossip.

Scholarships, Aid and Endowments

Scholarships aren't the only way to get "free money for college," but people sometimes confuse them with other methods like endowments and grants. So I want to take a moment to explain the differences for those of you who might not know.

What distinguishes most scholarships is the fact that they're based on merit. The applicant who best meets the decider's criteria – whether it's demonstrating achievement, writing a compelling essay or completing other requirements – is going to win. Some scholarships also take need into account, and only allow students below a specific income threshold to apply. However, once the threshold is met, those applicants are also judged against each other to determine who has the "best" application.

What's an Endowment?

Some colleges and universities offer help with tuition and fees to students who can't afford it based solely on how much they need it. That money comes from endowments – all the Ivy League schools and lots of other institutions have endowments, because they allow students with varied socioeconomic backgrounds to apply. Imagine what Harvard would look like if only students who could afford it went there and you'll get the idea.

So these schools subsidize a portion or even all of their students' tuition and fees at all different levels – and most provide at least some relief to middle income and even some upper income families. The money is awarded in the form of grants, loans and work/study programs, and the amount is based solely on need – if you're admitted to the school and you can demonstrate need, you get the money. Of course, if you want to avoid loans, you may want to do some research to find out how the schools you're applying to award their endowment money.

Regardless, this should also tell you that even if

your family income is low, you don't need to steer away from applying to expensive schools. Colleges are kind of like cars – they have a "sticker price" they publish in their guides and on their websites, but only a few people actually pay that price. So if the advertised price looks astronomical, that alone should not deter you from applying – the fees you're ultimately charged may be lower, and the scholarships you win may dramatically lower the final cost.

Grants

Exactly what your need *is* determined by the Free Application for Federal Student Aid, or FAFSA. The FAFSA is a U.S. Government form that uses your family's tax information and other financial data to figure out how much money you and your family can "officially" afford to pay for college – at least, according to government standards. If your family income is below a certain level, you'll be eligible for a government grant to help pay for school.

The income threshold for Federal aid is pretty low, and the amount you'll receive isn't usually enough to pay for a year at a state school, let alone a private one. However, even if you don't think you'll qualify for government money, filling out the FAFSA is still crucial because private colleges look at your FAFSA to determine how much endowment money you're entitled to. Since some schools offer help to students whose parents make up to six figures or more, it's definitely worth the time it takes to fill out.

It's also important to put some thought into *how* you fill out the FAFSA. You want to be as honest about your family's income as the law requires; however, you may not need to declare absolutely *everything*, so you want to leave out whatever you legally can to make that income appear as "competitive" as possible. This is not the time to overstate your income – this is one instance where less actually ends up being more (less income, more government aid).

That said, I'm not a tax expert, so I'm not qualified to give any specific advice beyond this: do your research. Ask an accountant or tax expert, fact check on the internet, make sure you know what you can legally skip reporting before you fill out your FAFSA and submit it to the government.

The availability of scholarships, endowments and grants all adds up to one important point – regardless of your family income, you don't need to put a limit on your dreams or restrict yourself to only community colleges or state schools. If you're concerned, you can go online and easily check how much endowment money any school you are interested in generally provides, and at what income levels. You'll probably be pleasantly surprised – while the "ticket price" may be unreachable, a lot of schools are actually much more affordable than you think. On the other hand, there are some very popular schools that have a pretty dismal record of offering financial aid. It's okay to apply there too – remember, you can win enough scholarships to pay for college – but if *all* the schools on your list are low on the aid scale, you might want to include one or two options that can serve as "financial safety schools." You can find "financial aid generous" schools online, or via conversations with current students or your counselor. Or do both – you can never have too much information.

What are Scholarship Orgs Looking For?

Now that we've dealt with all the possible ways to get money, let's switch our focus back to scholarships – they never involve loans, and a lot of them are available to you regardless of how much money your parents make, making them an ideal way to get help paying for college. Of course, in order to win a scholarship, you need to demonstrate that you are that stellar, amazing human being who deserves a scholarship even more than Mr. Spectacular. And there's a formula to doing that successfully.

Scholarships are, above all, a *business proposition.* The organizations that award them have specific reasons for giving that money away, and the reasons are as diverse as the organizations themselves. And that's exactly where the big opportunity lies for you.

A lot of applicants forget that the people reviewing scholarship applications are human beings, just like you. They aren't necessarily looking for someone who's perfect. They're looking for someone who embodies the ideals of their organization. So the more you appear like the ideal representation of what they're all about, the better your chance of winning a scholarship.

So...exactly how do you figure out how to "embody an organization's ideals?"

Look for the Mission Statement.

Every organization has a "mission statement" – if the specific scholarship you're applying for doesn't, which is rare, the organization offering the scholarship will. Find that mission statement (which isn't hard, it's usually right there on the website) and you'll be able to see, in black and white, exactly what they're looking for in a scholarship winner. Then you find the elements in your story that match up, and you emphasize them. If they're focused on growth, emphasize where you've grown. If they're focused on empowerment, emphasize the instances where you've empowered others. If they're focused on achievement, emphasize your accomplishments.

For example, here is the mission statement from the Coca-Cola Scholars Foundation website:

> *"What is our Mission? Provide scholarship programs and alumni enrichment opportunities in support of exceptional peoples' thirst for knowledge and their desire to make a difference in the world."*

If you look closely at the statement, you'll notice the phrase "exceptional people." So in your application, any essay you write and any materials you send, you'll want to show where you've been "exceptional" – where you've achieved more, or done more, or somehow distinguished yourself from the pack.

However, the most important phrase in this particular mission statement is "desire to make a difference in the world." The Coca-Cola Scholars Foundation is clearly looking to reward students who are doing or plan to do *something* to make the planet better. So on your application, you might give more attention to your outstanding record of community service than to your role on the varsity swim team. And if any of your career or life goals involve building houses for poor families or finding a cure for cancer, make sure to highlight those as well.

Remember, it's not about changing who you are or what you've done; it's about viewing yourself and your experiences through the scholarship board's eyes and tailoring your application to highlight the kinds of things they care about.

Give them what *they* want, and they'll give you what *you* want.

What Can You Do Now?

While scholarship committees ultimately will be looking for something specific, in a general sense, the vast majority are looking for the same thing – students who are engaged and interested and capable of achievement and success. So wherever you are in your high school career, there are things you can and should be doing right now to get ready to apply for – and win – scholarship money.

I'm going to start with freshmen and move from there, so if I'm covering material you already know, chill, skip ahead a few pages, and get ready. We'll be getting to you very soon.

If you are a freshman...

First of all, good for you. The fact that you're thinking about this now means you'll be way ahead of the game when the time for real work comes along. At this point, that time is a few years away, but there's still plenty you can do now to make sure you wind up positioned at the top of the heap.

Right now, you should be doing everything you can to excel in your classes. A history of high performance is a positive sign. However, that doesn't mean you should be signing up for easy classes because you know you'll easily "ace" them. Honors and AP (Advanced Placement) classes, and programs like International Baccalaureate (IB), are much more highly regarded, and weighted (for schools with weighted GPAs), giving students extra points for a more challenging course load.

The most important type of classes to consider is an AP class. These are college-level courses taught in high school, and if you pass the AP exam in your subject at the end of the school year, you can actually receive college credit for the class. This can be a very effective way of cutting college costs before you even start applying to schools – some colleges will award you credits for the AP classes you passed in high school, which can save you thousands of dollars. Some students are able to cut their expenses by a semester, or even a year.

One or two AP classes should be the limit freshman year – remember, you're just getting your feet wet, and since these are college-level classes, they can be very challenging. Overall, my advice for now is to do the best you can in the most challenging classes you can handle, and if you run into any trouble, get help immediately from your teacher or a tutor. Problem-solving will be a hugely important skill as you get older, so don't look into running into academic trouble as a negative; look at it as an opportunity to overcome something and to learn something (and add it to your story at some point down the line).

Outside the classroom, freshman year is time to start getting involved. Start attending club events and/or going out for different athletic teams or activities to find out what interests you most. Remember, there is no "right" organization to join. It's all about finding what you care about, and what you love to do, so you can start building a life around your passions.

If you are a sophomore...

Now is the time to start honing in on what you're good at – those classes you breezed through as a freshman and/or those subjects you're dying to know more about. If you're shy (or feel uncomfortable around adults or authority figures), now is the time to work on it. Building a rapport with your teachers is essential – you will need them in your corner later on, as part of what I call your "Board." Remember, they are there to help you do the very best you can, and most teachers would be thrilled to be consulted or asked about anything other than how to get a higher grade.

Ask your English teacher, or any other teacher you trust who deals with essay writing, for an honest assessment of where you are and where you can improve – this will be VERY important later on. Also, make sure you are signed up to take the PSAT standardized test through your school or district – ask at the beginning of the school year to make sure you don't miss it. Students who score especially well on the PSAT are automatically eligible for National Merit Scholarships.

Sophomore year is also the time to start taking the lead in certain areas – you can seek out leadership opportunities, and where people or organizations you care about may be looking for leaders, volunteer your services. I know this can be a challenge if you are introverted and are not looking to lead; however, remember that every great leader needs great people behind her...or him. You may not feel comfortable speaking in front of large crowds or instructing others on what to do, and if that describes you, that does not make you ANY less viable as a scholarship candidate. Remember, leadership is multidimensional – there are many ways to make yourself indispensable; your challenge is to find *your* way.

The most important thing you can do is find something an organization needs from you and provide it. Even if it's not a high-profile job, such as the "Official Facebook Ad Poster," the key is finding a way to fulfill an essential function. You're not just there to show up and get those community service hours counted on your record. You're there to contribute, to get something done, to make things better, and to develop a story to be used in an essay later on down the line.

If you are a junior...

Now is when things start getting serious. You're probably taking the hardest course load of your high school career, working hard on your essay technique, taking a handful of AP classes and studying for the SAT and ACT standardized tests. If you perform well on these tests, it can also lead to more money for college, plus most colleges require them when you apply – so don't skip them.

Hopefully you've also begun to receive some honors and accolades. If you haven't, make sure you're putting yourself out there, entering contests in areas where you are skilled – because you obviously aren't going to win anything if you don't try. And honors and awards really do help you stand out. So try everything – try to become the captain of your sports club, go out for leadership positions in student government and within any organizations you belong to, enter contests in art, drama, writing, science or anything you do well, actively seek out areas where you already know you excel and see what you can accomplish.

If there's nothing out there that feels like the right "fit," or even if you're just compelled to do it, start your own club or organization. This is the time to begin separating yourself from the pack, for concentrating on those areas that make *you* special, so think long and hard about who you are and what you want...and then make it happen.

Now is also a good time to start doing serious research on the types of schools you might want to attend, and believe it or not, you can even start applying to scholarships now. A lot of scholarships are available for Juniors – ask your counselor or Google "college scholarships for Juniors" to get started. If you find scholarships to apply for, be sure to skip ahead to the next chapters in this book for tips on how to fill out those applications successfully.

And of course, if you have any friends who are seniors, you'll want to pick their brains about any scholarships they've found, where they are looking and even the problems they are running into. Many schools start an online forum for the graduating senior class, and if your class has one, you can start posting your questions and/or answers there. If you don't have one, consider launching one – on your own, or with the help of a computer-savvy friend. It won't just give you a place to share tips and ideas and find answers to questions, it can also rank as a "community service" to your classmates and become part of your overall story.

If you are a senior...

Chances are, you aren't thinking about anything other than college, college, college right now. Okay, maybe the prom or the class trip, but once you hit Grade 12, you're bound to have college on the brain. By now, you should have already taken the ACT and/or SAT. You might want to take them a second time to see if you can boost your scores – they do tend to go up when you retake them.

Meet with your counselor as soon as you can (if you haven't already) and make it clear that you will be looking for scholarships. Your high school may have scholarships offered by affiliated organization or alumni, so ask your counselor if any exist and, if so, what steps you can take to be considered.

Don't worry about asking your counselor too many questions. Yes, you may get the sense that you are driving him or her insane, but helping you is actually your counselor's job! In fact, schools are judged by how many of their students go on to college, and when students go on to prestigious colleges, it reflects well on your school. So while your counselor will more than likely be busy, he or she should also be willing to help you and answer questions – you just may have to wait a day or two, so be firm, but also polite. And don't restrict your questions to your counselor – ask other students too. Again, an online forum is a great solution here, as students can often answer each other's questions on a lot of issues. If your school has a college bulletin board, be sure to check there.

Colleges applications start to become available in August, September and October – you'll want to use some of the techniques in this book – especially those focused on essay-writing and crafting your story – on your college applications. Plus, you may want to save some of the essays you write for your college apps to be "repurposed" later for scholarship applications. The bottom line is, get lots of opinions from experts, don't be afraid to edit, and keep copies of *everything*. But we'll get into that later.

The deadline for applying to scholarships varies greatly – in fact, you can be applying to scholarships year-round if you want to, so you'll want to be ready to switch your focus to scholarships the minute you're finished with your college applications. You should already be in the right mindset – positioning yourself as a candidate organizations will want to invest in.

Then it's time to move into the more specific steps you'll need to take to put together winning applications.

6 Keys to Unlock Greatness...

- Start thinking of your life as a "story" – look for the common threads running through your life experiences that show how far you've come and how you've done it.

- Familiarize yourself with the schools you might want to apply to and their financial aid programs.

- Make sure you are involved and engaged in your school and community.

- Actively seek out experiences and positions that will enrich your overall story.

- Get into the "Winning" Mindset. You are about to embark on a process that will require a huge commitment, continued resilience and prioritization. Limit excuses, and focus on finding ways to get things done.

- Visit www.educationalkeys.com for additional resources, group forums, scholarship commentary, and to post any questions you may have.

Section 2 – Build Your Board

Duck® brand duct tape's Stuck at Prom® Scholarship Contest offers college money to students who construct the best prom outfit out of duct tape. Entrants are judged according to how much Duck brand duct tape they use, as well as the originality and workmanship of their ensembles. The winning couple gets $5,000 each for college, the second place couple earns $3,000 each, third place nets the winners $2,000 apiece, and the remaining seven couples in the Top 10 win $500 each. The contest is open to all students over age 14 (including same-sex duos) who are attending a school-sanctioned high-school prom.

What is a Board and Why Do I Need One?

That's a very good question – well, actually two very good questions. So I'll take them on one at a time. Your Board consists of the very important people who you are going to enlist in your quest to earn scholarship dollars. They are the individuals who you will call on to help you get and send out whatever records or other information you need from your high school, to vouch for your greatness as a student or all-around human being, to help you craft the best scholarship applications possible and to generally offer advice and support through the whole "getting-into-and-paying-for-college" process.

Specifically, your Board has four unique roles – an Advisor, a Counselor, a Recommender and a Reviewer. You'll need at least one in each category, more in some, and one individual can play more than one role. For example, your Reviewer can also be a Recommender. But we'll get to those specifics later.

How do I set up this Board? In order to set up your Board, you need to be strategic; however, building these relationships is no different from how you would build relationships with other counselors or advisors.

Some high school students are totally focused on their relationships with their friends and classmates, which is completely normal. However, high school is also an important time to reach beyond your age group and start developing relationships with adults – specifically with people with influence, connections or information. The more types of people you know and associate with, the more experiences you'll have. And those experiences are a key part of your story.

You've probably heard the term "friends in high places." Well, for a young person just starting out, those kinds of friends are invaluable. If you have relationships with people who have influence, they can bend the rules for you, help you get special favors, and introduce you to other people and get them interested in who you are or what you do. This is called "networking," and the sooner you start doing it, the further you'll get in life. The network you develop now won't just help you win scholarships in the near future, but will help you get where you want to go in the decades to come.

All this talk about building relationships with powerful adults may have your head spinning – some students are totally comfortable in the adult world, but others, including some high achievers, are much more comfortable working on their own, writing, solving math problems or creating artistic masterpieces in private where no one can bother or distract them. That's all okay, that's part of what makes you unique and special and all that, but understand that at some point, you are going to need people. Your talents, even if they're amazing, will only get you so far in life – you need people in your corner to be your champion, to introduce you to other people who will recognize those talents and help you make the most of them. Otherwise, you could be the most amazing person in the world at whatever you do, but no one will know about it.

So if you're shy – and yes, I understand this might be difficult – now is the time to start getting yourself "out there."

You can definitely communicate with these "power players" on Facebook, Linkedin, Twitter, etc. since everyone uses them – there's no reason why you shouldn't. But, there's really no substitute for good, old-fashioned face-to-face interaction, where you can look somebody in the eye and tell them, "This is who I am and this is what I'm all about." Face time means something. It tells people you're a serious person worth investing their time in. So try to focus on those few teachers or other adults you feel most comfortable with so that you can fill the roles you're going to need for your Board.

Your "Elevator Pitch"

One easy and effective way to briefly and clearly explain who you are is with what is known as your "elevator pitch." This is a brief and to-the-point summary of You and Your Potential that you memorize and deliver in about 30 seconds – or the amount of time you might spend riding an elevator with a mover-shaker (hence the name...clever, right?). This pitch will be incredibly important during interviews as it will keep you focused on your story and eliminate any need to fumble around for words. However, it's never too early to start creating and refining yours.

This is a sample elevator pitch. And yes, full disclosure here: it was *my* elevator pitch. It should give you an idea of how an elevator pitch is constructed.

> *"I'm the president of a 30-person student organization called Youth Empowerment Program, and we've raised $3,000 for winter coats this year. I'm passionate about ensuring all youth have the essential household items, like shelter, coats and gloves, so I've spent the last year working with YEP and school administration to raise awareness about disadvantaged youth. I volunteer at the local Salvation Army, speak out at community events, and I'm excited to tell you more about my interests and goals."*

Whatever your specific experiences, skills, and interests are, this basic formula should help you construct a killer elevator pitch.

Sentence 1:

Lead with your biggest accomplishment and briefly sum up details – this will be the **theme** of your pitch. Use numbers (30-member, $3,000) since they are quantifiable indicators of achievement.

Sentence 2:

Next, briefly expand on your theme by explaining what you care about and why you've focused on that particular area. Finish that sentence with more general info about things you've been doing in that area.

Sentence 3:

List a few more accomplishments that relate to your theme and end by expressing interest in talking to the "pitch-ee" (that person) further. Make sure to be specific about why you have chosen this person to talk to: "I am very passionate about community service and your role as YMCA Director seems to directly line up with my interests. I think you could be an incredible resource to me as I continue to pursue my goals"

And you're done!

Your Advisor

Your Advisor is probably the most important person on your Board, because he or she will be your cheerleader and your anchor – and the person who helps you through your transition from high school to college. Advisors help you remain on schedule by providing you encouragement during the tough times, reviewing your application materials, helping you brainstorm ways to make your applications stand out, and basically serving as "You" advocates. For instance, my Advisor helped me improve my resume and find scholarships, and he reached out to others on my behalf to advocate for me obtaining a leadership position within an organization.

The right Advisor can be instrumental in helping you construct your "story" and build the kind of high school record that will showcase your strengths and present you as the standout individual that you know you are. Later, your Advisor can help you decide what kind of colleges you want to apply to and even strategize with you on specific scholarships to focus on.

When choosing your Advisor, make sure it is someone who you believe has wisdom to share and can help point you in the right direction. Make sure the person fully understands the level of commitment necessary and the expecations you have of an Advisor.

Someone you identify who knows you, believes

in you and is willing to take time out of his or her busy schedule to help you, can be your Advisor. A lot of students expect their guidance counselor to fill this role, and a lot of counselors do...to varying degrees. And if your counselor has the time and the interest, he or she may be an ideal choice.

However, I made Counselor a separate position on your Board for a reason. If you go to a larger high school, your counselor may be working with hundreds of students that are just as inquisitive as you are about college and scholarships, never mind all the associated forms to mail out and deadlines to meet. As much as your counselor may want to help you, there might not be enough hours in the day for your counselor to give you the kind of personal attention you need. Additionally, counselors do not always check up on you to make sure you're meeting those scholarship deadlines – and even those who do probably won't make sure you're writing the kind of creative opening statements that will captivate your audience!

That's why your best move may be to find an Advisor who is not your counselor to help you formulate a plan for your immediate future and fill in wherever your counselor may not be able to help.

A teacher you've really clicked with during high school is a great choice, especially if the future path you want to pursue has something to do with the subject he or she teaches. But even that isn't necessary as long as this is a teacher who really feels strongly about you and your future. If you have any adult mentors outside of school – maybe a member of a charity you volunteer at or a family friend who is well-connected in the education or business world – these would also make good Advisors.

Friends and peers don't make the best Advisors, even if you trust them, even if they're brilliant. The key is, you want your Advisor to be someone who knows more than you, who has been there before, who has connections in the outside world or outside your bubble and can offer the kind of guidance you can't find on your own. While there is definitely a huge role for your friends in your scholarship search, relying only on your peers will rob you of an adult perspective – something that really helps when you're entering the adult world.

How Do You Get An Advisor?

If you're one of those students who has a lot of strong relationships with teachers, administrators and other adults, choosing an Advisor will just be a matter of deciding who is the best "fit" for you, and then – and this is the important part – making sure that person is willing and able to fill the role. Don't just assume that the person you've chosen to advise you has the time or desire to actually *be* your Advisor. Plus, people feel good when they're asked to do things, so schedule some time for a face-to-face meeting to pop the question, to discuss your plans, your goals, and most importantly, why you want to work with them. If you can go into this meeting with items written down and show some proactive stance taken on your end, it will speak to your seriousness and position you as a person worth investing time in.

I'm not trying to imply that you should be at all nervous or afraid about asking someone to be your Advisor. Especially people in the education field – they live for students who care about school and their future. They like to feel important and are comforted knowing their work actually means something since the day-to-day grind of trying to educate six classes full of kids who would rather be home texting their boyfriends while watching "Jersey Shore" can suck the life out of them. So chances are, teachers or administrators will be overly enthused by your request to join your Board as an Advisor. It may even make someone's day.

However, a word of caution – there's nothing more frustrating than deciding on an Advisor and learning at some point down the line that he or she doesn't really have the time for you. Most students don't feel comfortable coming down on teachers, or any adults other than their parents, for items that are pressing to them. So try to be as honest and upfront as you can be about the kind of time you'll need. And if your favorite teacher is a flake, understand that he or she might not be the best choice for an Advisor. Or understand you're going to have to take a little more responsibility to manage the relationship.

When you do decide on a potential Advisor who agrees to work with you, it's your job to not just listen to the advice, but to decide on your own what aspects of the advice are applicable to your life. Your Advisor is there to offer advice – he or she isn't God. He or she is there to help you shape your future, but remember to focus on the word "help." If something doesn't feel right, if you feel pushed in a direction you don't feel comfortable going, it is okay to talk about why you feel uncomfortable and what you'd prefer. Your Advisor can be a springboard for some interesting discussions about you and how an outsider perceives your abilities, so stay open, but stay honest about your own likes and dislikes, hopes and dreams.

Once you've enlisted an Advisor, it's also important to make some time to meet with them and actually get that expert advice. Plan in advance and schedule lunch or an after-school meeting to catch up and go over whatever is going on at the time. Confirm those meetings in advance, and – this should go without saying – show up on time, be prepared, and always thank them for their help.

Word of caution on enlisting an Advisor – you wouldn't ask a girl to be your girlfriend on your first date (at least I hope not). Similarly, you shouldn't ask someone that you just met to be your Advisor on Day 1 either. Let the relationship develop naturally, and when you think it's evolved to the right place, spring it on your would-be Advisor in a planned and well thought out manner – in other words, make an offer he or she can't refuse.

Oh – and bringing homemade cookies to the first meeting is a nice touch.

Your Counselor

Your Counselor is the only member of your Board you don't have to choose – he or she has already been hired to work for you.

Well, you and possibly a few hundred other people just like you.

Generally, your Counselor is your go-to person for all the administrative things you'll need when you apply to college and scholarships – things like making you aware of various application deadlines, handling transcript requests and signing fee waivers (if you qualify for reduced fees on the SAT, ACT or college applications) and just generally getting all the "official" information about you to the organizations you're applying to. They may also provide you with compiled lists of scholarships on local and national organizations you can apply to. Some offices may have rules that require them to submit scholarship applications on your behalf.

The majority of guidance Counselors do more than push your official papers in the right direction. They provide help with things like choosing the right classes, deciding what colleges might be a good fit and even understanding your financial aid options.

The tricky part is your Counselor may be doing

those same things for a lot of people. So the best way to get the most out of your Counselor is to make it as easy as possible for them to help you. Schedule regular meetings ahead of time if you can, don't wait until the last minute, and ask what works best with his or her schedule. Get as much information as you can on your own, network with your friends, and ask your Advisor, before you and your Counselor meet. If you can start at Square Three instead of Square One, it will make a huge difference.

For instance, if your school requires that your Counselor mail out all of your scholarship applications, go into your Counselor's office with the envelope already addressed and stamped, with one of those little sticky notes that says "sign here." The more prep work you can do on your own, the more likely it is that your Counselor will feel good about working with you and actually look forward to seeing your face in his or her doorway. Remember, it might be the Counselor's job, but it's YOUR future.

Your Counselor will also be the person who lets you know if your school has any set deadlines in the application process or has a limit on the number of transcript requests you can make. Make sure you ask him or her how your particular school handles the scholarship process. If your school deals with official transcript requests, ask if you can have a few extras to hang onto in case a last-minute deadline or opportunity creeps in.

Some Counselors will work with you very specifically to help develop a financial aid plan. These Counselors are aware of the schools that have the biggest endowments and give the most money to students, which community colleges and state schools provide aid, and what school awards might be available to you. Some high schools even offer their own scholarships to students who meet different criteria, like excellence in sports, service or a specific subject.

Remember, your Counselor is your only Board member whom, even if your relationship is a total disaster, you're going to be stuck with for the rest of your high school career. So it's crucial that you find the most productive, positive, and helpful way to deal with your Counselor, as he or she plays a role in getting you where you want to go. Be clear and firm about your needs, but don't freak out, don't yell, and please don't cry. And if all else fails, turn to someone else on the school staff who you trust will help get what you need.

Also, remember what I said about the cookies.

4 Keys to a Relationship with your Counselor

- Make sure to ask your Counselor to clarify your school's particular application process and take time to familiarize yourself with any policies and requirements.

- Keep copies of everything – transcripts, letters of recommendation, and lists of extracurricular activities, community service projects, social organizations and internships. You don't want to have to keep going back and asking for the same things over and over again. Being organized means that you are serious.

- Trick yourself into never missing a deadline by setting a "personal deadline" on yourself two weeks in advance. This will give you plenty of time to review application materials and deal with last-minute changes – and avert disaster if any surprise issues pop up. By revisiting your completed application a few times after it's "finished," you can find sneaky hidden errors, sharpen your story and generally keep improving your application until it really shines.

- Help your Counselor by doing as much of the administrative part of the job as you can. If your school requires copies of all materials, bring those copies to your Counselor. If he or she has to mail your completed application, bring pre-addressed envelopes and stamps. Make your Counselor's life easier, and he or she will do the same for you.

Your Reviewer

I just talked about allowing some time to work and rework your application until it's as close to perfect as you can get it. However, this is not a process you want to go through entirely on your own. The last thing in the world you want to do is turn in an essay with typos or misspellings – and it's also good to know that your essay makes sense to someone other than you. So to make sure your essays and any other written materials are ready for submission, you'll need at least one Reviewer – and possibly more than one.

A Reviewer's job is to read through your application materials with the idea of helping you improve them in terms of grammar and content. Your Reviewer should be the person with the best command of English that you know – English teachers are a natural, but not necessary, choice – who can offer you clear guidance, reasoned judgment and constructive criticism. If you can, choose a Reviewer who already knows your writing strengths and understands the story you're trying to communicate through your application – this can add a lot of value to your application. However, you also need your Reviewer to be unbiased and honest. You don't just want to be told how great your essay is (so leave Mom and Dad out, unless you're confident they know their stuff). You want real, concrete, specific advice on how to improve your application.

A Reviewer's job isn't as demanding as that of an Advisor – the process of reading and commenting on an essay can take a few minutes to an hour or two, depending on how many pages you've written. However, you'll want to be sure whoever you ask to look over your work has enough time to devote some undivided attention to helping you. Also, never give a Reviewer an essay or piece of writing to review at the last minute – that's a lot of pressure on them, and not smart for you as a rushed Reviewer may miss something or not do the best job. Give each Reviewer at least a week, and check in midway through to make sure they still have the time to review your work. The "check in" should be a courteous reminder. You can do it in the form of an email – thanking them for being vested in your future first and then noting the deadline – or show off those fancy baking skills with another batch of cookies. Just remember to reach out in the nicest way possible. If not, thank them for trying and find a replacement. Do not get into a situation where everyone and their brother offers an opinion of your essay, but two or three insightful pairs of eyes may be better than one.

Have your Reviewer(s) address the following:

• Style	• Citations
• Content	• Vocabulary
• Organization	• Theme consistency
• Grammar	• Spelling

And also ask them these 3 key questions:

- If I take my name off this essay, would it sound like it could just as easily be an essay by Jane Doe or

Mr. Spectacular, or does it sound like it comes from a unique individual?

- If you were on the scholarship committee, would you recommend awarding me the funds based on this essay? Why or why not?

- Can you point out two strong points and two areas where I can improve?

Another word about Mom and Dad, or anyone else who knows you well – it might be good to have at least one person who is aware of and understands your "story" on your list of reviewers, because he or she will be able to tell if you're leaving out important points or downplaying your achievements.

Another Key!

From an organization that has awarded over $2 million dollars in scholarships...

> "Students generally work on essays so much that they fail to catch the small typos and misuse of words such as advice vs. advise. Avoid this by rereading your essays out loud in 18" font, because the huge font forces you

to read every word."

Your Recommender

Most scholarship applications require one or two letters of recommendation. It's important for scholarship committees to see some evidence that you truly are the amazing, incredible person you say you are, and letters of recommendation play an essential role by providing an extra measure of credibility.

A good Recommender will do more than detail the same accomplishments you'll have listed on your scholarship applications. He or she will have something to say about the person you are and what makes you unique, and why he or she believes that you are an ideal recipient of the scholarship. Since scholarship boards will be focusing a lot of attention on what your Recommender has to say (after all, they asked for the recommendation), it's important that whoever you choose will provide the strongest possible argument on your behalf.

Because of this, when you look for a Recommender, there are two ideals to aim for. One is to get a recommendation from a person with clout or status – your school principal, the head of a local organization, someone whose title will impress the scholarship committee, or even better, someone with some connection to the organization you're applying to. The other is to find a Recommender who has worked with you closely in some capacity and knows you well, like a favorite teacher or advisor. Since you'll likely need two recommendations, try to line up one of each if you can, but note: the **Most Important Thing** is that a Recommender knows and can speak to your story. For example, if Bill Gates wrote me a recommendation, but all it said was "Marvis is smart," I don't think it would do much.

You'll also want to try to find Recommenders who are willing to collaborate with you. If you can tell your Recommender what your story is, what you want to highlight and the overall picture you're trying to paint, and get the Recommender to work with you to make sure the right story gets told, you'll be in an ideal situation.

Some Recommenders will actually ask you to write the letter for them and just give it back for them to sign. What you do here really depends on how much you want this particular person to be part of your application as well as your personal ethics, but I personally don't recommend it. A good recommender will write things about you that you might never think to say about yourself – he or she will provide an outsider's perspective, an adult perspective, which is something you really can't do on your own. So unless you really can't find anyone willing to sit down and write a few lines about you, I would try to limit your involvement to providing some basic guidance about the story you're trying to tell.

Then there are other Recommenders who fall more on the other end of the spectrum and try to limit your involvement. This is not necessarily a bad thing – you can get an amazing recommendation without having any input at all if you choose the right Recommender. You just want to make sure your recommender understands what the scholarship committee is looking for, and that he or she will reinforce your theme and sing your praises without reservation.

On that note, you should ALWAYS provide your Recommenders with plenty of information on your theme: a copy of your scholarship essay, resume, portfolio, academic history, and other "talking points" that they can use for reference. If there's a specific story you want mentioned, you can guide your Recommender in that direction (for example, "please be sure to say something like, 'After I encouraged Harry to continue his passion for helping youth through community outreach, he organized the school's first annual coat drive, collecting over 100 coats and $3,000 of donations for disadvantaged youth in our community.'")

If your Recommender is okay with you reviewing the letter, be sure to check it for typos as well as the bigger thematic and structural issues. Regardless, remember to allow your Recommender plenty of time to write your letter. Don't give a Recommender a last-minute deadline; think about using that two-week "personal deadline" we talked about earlier to allow you time to deal with any unforeseen disasters, like a recommendation letter that says you're actually kind of a jerk. This doesn't happen often, but if it does, you want to be ready! And once you have your letter in your hot little hands, be sure to keep a few signed and sealed copies in your file for any last-minute scholarships that might spring up.

Remember, strong letters of recommendation don't just sing your praises without providing details. Insiders say that they tend to not believe a letter of support that doesn't provide material to back up the letter. So try to be sure there are concrete examples, such as,

> "In my ten years teaching, I have yet to meet another student as motivated as Harry. After planning a breast cancer walk for several months, he solicited support from the principal and other school administrators alongside securing $4,000 for cancer research."

Notice how the facts and figures affirm the praise given by the recommender. Examples are essential evidence you will need in order to validate the claims made in your letters of recommendation – so encourage your Recommenders to include them when you recruit them to write on your behalf.

Here are some final keys on choosing the right Recommender:

- Choose someone who taught you in class and can speak to your strengths as a student.

- Choose someone from a class where you were very visible and participated in projects and discussions.

- Choose someone who you already know is enthusiastic about you and your cause.

- Ask any would-be Recommenders honestly if they have the available time and if they believe that they can write a strong letter. This gives them an out if they don't think they can sincerely endorse you.

- If possible, choose someone who is willing to work with you on the letter.

- This may go without saying, but choose a recommender who can write well. If your calculus teacher thinks you're a genius, but barely speaks a word of English, you might want to look elsewhere. Unfortunately, bad writing skills can undermine any good things a Recommender says about you.

- Choose a recommender you can trust to meet your deadlines.

Now that you have an idea of how to get your Board in place, let's get ready to move onto the challenges ahead. Here are some thoughts about what you should be doing right now to make this process as seamless and rewarding as possible.

If you are a freshman...

This year is all about meeting people, making connections and starting to figure out who you are and what you want. Now is the time to meet with your Counselor, if already assigned to you, to talk about your strengths, interests and goals. Yes, these will change over time, but the sooner you start making choices with a specific plan in mind, the more significant experiences you'll have to address on your scholarship applications later on. Your Counselor will likely be more than happy to help you create an education plan designed to get you somewhere special in life. If your Counselor has not been assigned to you, start enlisting any teachers you click with in this cause. Remember: don't be intimidated – most educators will be more than happy to help an enthusiastic, caring student. Talk about your goals and dreams, get them involved – you might be surprised how many people take an interest in you and your cause. If your Counselor has not been assigned, meet with one that's available.

If you are a sophomore...

Meet with your Counselor again, possibly at a few points during the year, to make sure you're on track academically. Also, make sure you're building the relationship naturally. Relationships are mutual, so it's nice if you express some interest in your Counselor as a human being, not just a person whose sole purpose on Earth is to do things for you.

At this point, you're probably starting to gravitate more towards subjects you're skilled in, and meeting more teachers who like what you like in the process and getting more involved with them. Keep this up. You'll also probably be involved in some types of organizations by now – service, sports, extracurriculars, that sort of thing. Whatever you're doing with your spare time is likely something you feel passionate about, so look to develop relationships with your adult advisors as well.

This may be the point in high school where "social temptations" start to kick in. Keep your eyes on the prize and remember, you may stumble now and then, you may not always get straight A's, but you do need to keep your house in order to keep people on your side! And yes, if you're wondering, this applies in every grade.

If you are a junior...

It's time to start thinking about college, so be sure to catch up with your Counselor to make sure you're progressing towards your goals and narrowing down a list of colleges to focus your attention on. Continue to build relationships with your teachers and advisors. Keep them updated on your goals and successes, as well as the schools you're thinking of and the areas you'd like to study. There are a lot of free online resources to help you hone in on your character and personal interests. If you're emerging as a leader and fulfilling an integral role in an organization, be sure to spend some quality time with your advisor discussing the impact you're having on the organization and how you might build on that. These leadership experiences will later become the subject of future essays.

If you are a senior...

You'll likely spend a lot of time with your Counselor this year preparing college and scholarship applications. If you haven't already, choose the rest of your Board members, and set up meetings with each one – make time every quarter to meet formally with the ones you don't see regularly. Try to stay calm and focused – the application process can add a lot of pressure and take up a lot of time, especially if you're already busy with AP classes and extracurriculars. One way to keep it all under control is to stay organized – then there will be no need to panic looking for that missing application, essay, or even transcript...

Now take a deep breath and get ready – it's time to go find some money!

Section 3 – Find Funding

The Patrick Kerr Skateboard Scholarship is open to all high school seniors who are U.S. citizens, have an unweighted GPA of at least 2.5, and most importantly, love to skateboard. Applicants must write a short essay on "how skateboarding has been a positive influence in their life." The first place winner is awarded $5,000, and three runners-up receive $1,000 each (to be used at an accredited two or four-year college or university).

Search Overview

By now, you know that there are literally millions – *millions* – of scholarship dollars out there just waiting to be claimed by deserving students like you. But figuring out where and how to find these scholarships can be a little overwhelming. It's not that scholarships are hard to find – they aren't hiding anywhere. The problem is really the opposite. There's so much information about so many scholarships that it can become overwhelming, and even unbearable. So in this chapter, I'll attempt to demystify the process and help you formulate a plan to research your options one step at a time.

Complete the FAFSA

I already mentioned the FAFSA – the Free Application for Federal Student Aid. You can find it on the Government's website, fafsa.ed.gov, along with the basic instructions for filling it out.

I'm also going to mention again – because it is *that* important – that even if you think your parents make "too much money," you still need to complete the FAFSA. The reason? The FAFSA doesn't just determine if you're eligible for U.S. Government assistance, which includes grants, work-study programs, and federal student loans with fixed interest rates. It also helps colleges determine the amount of financial aid to award you.

So unless your dad is Bill Gates (in which case, I'm flattered you're reading this book), yes, you need to fill out your FAFSA.

After you do, you will receive a Student Aid Report (SAR) specifying how much money you and your family can "officially" afford to pay for college, called your EFC (Estimated Financial Contribution). Depending on how much you need, you may qualify for government grants including the Pell Grant, which provides a maximum of $5,500 per year, the Federal Supplemental Educational Opportunity Grant, which provides a maximum of $4,000, and if you are a veteran, the Iraq and Afghanistan Service Grant of $5,500. There are also federal grants of varying amounts for students who plan to teach. (Figures are as of 2012).

However, even if you don't qualify for a grant, the FASFA can still help by giving you access to federal, low-interest student loans including:

- Perkins, which provides up to $5,500 per year

- Direct Stafford, which allows you to borrow up to $31,000 over four years of college, including up to $5,500 for your first year, $6,500 for the second year, $7,500 for the third year and whatever's left-over out of $31,000 for the fourth.

- Direct PLUS loans, which allows you to borrow the remaining cost of attendance after any other aid you receive

Ideally, once you're through with this book, you won't need a loan. However, just knowing you qualify is great as a backup measure. Which is probably why almost 15 million people fill out the FASFA every year.

Of course, *how* you fill out that FAFSA will have a lot to do with what the FAFSA can ultimately do for you. The following keys will ensure you present the best possible picture of your financial state – and by best possible, I mean lowest – to Uncle Sam.

First of all, if your parents are not together, you're in luck! You only have to report one of their incomes (as long as you've spent time living with both) – and if one of your parents makes less money than the other, you only need to report that lower income. And you thought having two Christmases was great...

Second, TMI (too much information) is a bad thing when it comes to the FAFSA. You don't have to report all of your family's income – although you may want to check with a tax expert for specifics if your parents have a lot of assets. However, you don't have to report your home (at least not the one you live in most of the time, Bill Gates Jr.) or farm, a business with less than 100 employees, 401 (k) plans, retirement plans, non-education IRAs, annuities, life insurance or pension funds. You will need to report any other real estate (that means you again, Bill), 529 college savings plans and Coverdell savings accounts, trust funds, UGMA and

UTMA accounts, money market funds, certificates of deposit, stocks, stock options and bonds.

Another hint: you're required to list your family's assets as of the day you sign your FAFSA. Which means, if your family has any big bills coming up, empty that bank account first and then file. If you're expecting a big tax refund or think you might be winning the lottery in the near future, file now before that cold, hard cash comes rolling in.

If you work, you will have to declare the money you make. But don't worry, unless you're working full time or are one of those child prodigy entrepreneurs, there's almost no chance your income will make much of a difference. So you can keep your after-school job.

Scholarships

Now we've come to the good stuff. The most the FAFSA can bring you is a few thousand dollars, which probably won't be enough to cover your costs at an in-state school. With scholarships, however, the money you can bring in is basically unlimited, meaning you can even wind up with enough cash to finance trips home for the holidays. So whatever you think about your potential for getting help from the government or endowments, you cannot lose if you conduct a thoughtful, thorough scholarship search.

Yes, I said "thoughtful" and "thorough." The reason a lot of students find scholarship searches so frustrating is that they take on the task of searching through thousands and thousands of scholarships without a plan. If you're going to find the right scholarships for you and make sure you're not missing anything, you need to approach this step by step.

Step 1: Get Organized

The first step is to plan in advance how you will organize the information you uncover. Maybe it will be stored in a spreadsheet on your laptop or even, if you're old-school, on paper. Just do it, invest the time, create the file, make the folder, buy the binder, have it with you whenever you search. You'll want to record the following information for every scholarship that interests you:

- Scholarship name/link/contact info

- Amount of money awarded

- Deadline

- Any specific requirements (essay, subject specific, etc.)

- Contacts

- Progress and response date

Treat this seriously now and I promise, you'll thank me later!

Go to www.educationalkeys.com *to download a sample Excel spreadsheet to help you stay organized.*

My System

You don't have to do it this way, but if you're looking for a concrete example, this is how I kept everything organized...and managed to apply to 72 scholarships within a single year.

I bought a one-inch binder, 14 tabs, and a set of clear page dividers. I organized it by due date, using a tab for each month, plus one for essays and one for additional material. I used one clear page divider for each scholarship, and added my notes on requirements, due dates and any other relevant information. And I packed it with as many scholarships as I could find.

An alternative to this would be to create an Excel sheet, and have it always accessible via computer, flashdrive, or cloud file-storing software, e.g. Dropbox. This ensures you're always working from the most current version.

And don't worry, we'll devise a strategy to prioritize which scholarships to apply to later, but for now, you want to cast a wide net.

Step 2: Go to Your Info Sources

Okay, now that you're ready to go, let's approach the different sources of scholarship information step by step.

1. **Your School**

Your high school is the natural best place to start your scholarship search. If your school has a college bulletin, you should check it frequently for scholarship announcements.

If you're a senior, your Counselor probably has a lot of information about state and local scholarships ready for you and your classmates right now. He or she may even be able to suggest some scholarships that will be a good fit for you specifically.

Just remember that your Counselor is likely also doing this for a few hundred other students – so don't make him or her responsible for your entire scholarship search. Use whatever your Counselor provides as a launching point, and go on from there. Even if he or she provides you with a long list of scholarships, there is a lot of information that won't be there, and some of what's missing could be what's best for you. So don't be lazy!

That said, some high schools really do make it almost ridiculously easy. I know of a school in Southern California that makes a huge production of awarding scholarships to their top achievers – they have a big scholarship dinner at the end of the year and present awards, giving away hundreds of thousands of dollars. If your school is one of these, you probably already know about it – but there's still no harm in asking your

Counselor about such an event just to be 100% certain.

This school in California – a normal, public high school, btw – gives awards ranging from a few hundred dollars to a few thousand to the top students across the different departments including Spanish, English, Math, and even across student organizations, athletics, and community service. Some alumni, local businesses and organizations also give their own scholarships at the dinner.

But here's the really amazing part. Earlier in the year, the school gives all seniors who request it a "scholarship package" that they can fill out with their information to make it easier for the school to match them with scholarships – including those in the local community! Which is why you really should check and see if your school offers anything like this – as you can imagine, it can be a huge help.

2. **Your Local Area**

On the other hand, if your school doesn't offer anything like what I just described, you're not out of luck. You can provide yourself with access to just as many great scholarships by doing some research. And by research, I of course mean some serious Googling.

Because they choose their winners from a smaller pool, local scholarships can offer great odds of landing scholarship dollars – although those dollar figures are generally lower than those you'll find at a national level. To find scholarships in your area, start by Googling your city, town or region – whatever it's locally referred to as – plus the word "scholarships." If you can think of a national organization, try typing your city plus that organization to see if it offers a local scholarship. For instance, if you Google NFIB, National Federation of Independent Business, you'll be directed to the organization's national scholarship. But if you add the name of your city, your local chapter, which may offer its own scholarship, will come up. If you know of any businesses that are prominent in your town or area, you can also check their websites to find out if they offer scholarships. Furthermore, local governments, city councils and boards as well as local university campus organizations may set up scholarships for students. Be sure to check those out as well.

If you get tired of the computer and want to expand your search, you can always browse newspapers, books and articles or visit the library, neighboring churches and credit unions for leads. All of these are great resources to complement your online search. However, for the most information, you'd be wise to start with the online databases like finaid.com, fastweb, scholarships.com, and other sites that compile large amounts of relevant scholarship information into a single resource.

3. **Your State**

Some states, including Arizona, Arkansas, Florida, Georgia, Indiana and Louisiana, have special programs providing tuition waivers for state colleges. The requirements are different in each state, so Google yours to find out – even if your state doesn't offer a waiver, there may be other scholarships or awards offered. Just browse your state's .gov page and search "scholarships." You could also search your state-specific scholarships through Google using "your state" and "scholarships" in the search field

Not that I'm assuming you don't know how to Google – I'd just would rather keep this as clear as possible and eliminate any potential confusion for Bill Jr., or anyone else who might get lost.

4. **Your Interests**

Here is where a smart, creative scholarship-seeker can really cash in. Whatever you do, whatever you love, whatever you're good at, even something as simple as who you are – there's an app for that. A scholarship application, that is.

Remember the skateboard scholarship at the beginning of this chapter? There are hundreds more like it, for everyone from champion bowlers to amazing essay writers to science geeks. I'm showing you just a handful in this book – but I'm doing it to make a point. There are scholarships for everybody, not just the Mr. Spectaculars of the world. And the scholarships that have a special connection to you, that are offered to people like you, are the ones you have the best chance of winning.

To find them – I swear, this will be the last time I mention this – Google your passion, interests and skills, with the word "scholarship."

Now I will no longer insult your intelligence.

College money based on your passion or skill doesn't always come in official "scholarship" form. If you excel in a particular field such as science, law, etc., you can also look for competitions to enter. What's especially great about these competitions is that many of them allow you to enter projects you're probably completing for school anyway – things like student films or science fair projects – and use them to gain national recognition and college funding. Ask your teachers and counselor if they're aware of any of these competitions, or Google your interest or skill to see if there are any local or national competitions you can enter.

As an example (and for a little inspiration), these four competitions are probably the most prestigious in the world for high school students who are aspiring scientists, engineers, etc.

Intel International Science and Engineering Fair ($75,000 Top Award & over $4 million in Overall Awards): www.societyforscience.org/isef/ is the world's largest pre-college science competition.

Intel Science Talent Search ($100,000 Top Award): www.intel.com/about/corporateresponsibility/education/sts/index.htm

Siemens Competition (Awards range from

$1,000 to $100,000): www.siemens-foundation.org/

Junior Science & Humanities Symposium ($12,000 Top Award): www.jshs.org/

One more important tip in this area – if you know what you plan to study in college, there are also hundreds of thousands of scholarship dollars awarded to people who want to pursue careers in just about every field, including business, science, nursing and math. Don't feel like you have to be 100 percent committed to majoring in that area of study – as long as you're more than 50% confident that's the direction you'll go in, don't be afraid to apply. Over 70% of students enter college with one very popular major – Undeclared. Even if you're one of that very decisive 30% who knows what you're going to do, keep in mind that most college students do change their major frequently before making a final decision.

The important decision you need to make right now is to start looking and building your list. The amount of money you can find and potentially win is really only limited by your time, drive and your imagination.

5. **Your College**

In addition to the need-based grants I mentioned a few chapters ago, many colleges and universities also offer scholarships to students who meet specific criteria. This can be anything from demonstrated leadership, excellence in sports (in some cases, a school's entire football or basketball team can be on scholarship!), academic excellence and occasionally more obscure requirements that may fit the whims of the alumni who fund the awards.

Your high school "pedigree" is likely to matter here – the more great stuff you've done, the higher the chance you'll be singled out for this type of award. So remember this and remember your story in the essays you write, in the extracurricular activities you include on your application, in pretty much everything you do.

Within reason, of course.

Schools generally prepare their financial aid award letters after you've been admitted, so unless the school specifically advertises institutional awards on their site, like Stanford's and Harvard's free tuition programs for low-income students, do not assume you are or are not eligible for these types of scholarships. The best thing you can do is reach out to the school's Financial Aid office and confirm you're being considered for institutional grants and alumni scholarships.

You don't have to search the internet or anyplace else for these scholarships – the Financial Aid office finds you. Sometimes, you can even receive a scholarship from your school without knowing or doing anything about it. When I was accepted to Cornell University, I was selected for a scholarship without applying because the materials I had sent to the school demonstrated what they considered a high level of leadership in high school. So think carefully when you choose your next college application essay topic – you may wind up earning more than just admission.

6. National Organizations

Most of the biggest scholarships in America are awarded by national organizations – businesses, philanthropies, causes, foundations and even some very well-off individuals and families. The Big Daddy of them all – that pays for all of your schooling up to a Ph.D. – is the Bill and Melinda Gates Millennium Scholarship. There are hundreds of other well-known awards including the U.S. Rhodes Scholarship, Coca Cola Scholar's Foundation and countless others, all from large organizations and companies that want to promote good corporate stewardship by awarding deserving students cash for school.

Some of these scholarships are reserved for descendents and family members of employees, so be sure to compile a list of both companies that your family and friends work for and associations to which they belong to see if you're eligible for these exclusive scholarships.

If your family and friends aren't part of the corporate world, that's okay too. Google is the best way to find the widest range of scholarships – you can search any category that aligns with your theme and fits your mold. Some give you the chance to be creative, design videos, prepare PowerPoints, write stories...others ask that you do some form of creative writing, while still others are more straightforward. Spend some time exploring their websites, bounce ideas off your Board, and apply to as many scholarships as you believe you're strongly qualified for. The more applications you fill out, the greater your chances of success.

Be warned: while you are looking over a scholarship site online, you might click on a link that looks promising, and suddenly be faced with a request for credit card information. When that happens, don't reach for Mom's wallet just yet. Many fee-for-service scholarship sites are completely legit, but with everything you already know, chances are you really don't need them. If you want to pay some outside entity to search for you, do some research to make sure you'll get more for your money than you would be getting on your own – paying for the same list of scholarships you can find on Google is a huge waste of money, especially with the prom, grad night and all the rest of those senior expenses coming up.

So be smart – look for any online reviews or complaints about any service you're considering, get confirmation on exactly what they offer, look for some sort of guarantee, ask your Board members what they think. And if it all looks good, go ahead and grab Mom's Visa.

Just be sure to ask first.

What You Should Be Doing Now

If you are a freshman...

You really need to be thinking about ways in which you can distinguish yourself in your high school career to earn scholarships. If you get the opportunity, you might want to familiarize yourself with your Counselor's office and any scholarship programs your school may offer, so you can incorporate a winning strategy into your four-year plan. Remember, you're just starting to build the story that is going to win you multiple scholarships a few years down the line, so you should be concentrating your efforts in that arena. But it is always important to work with the end in mind. It might be a good idea to pick five scholarships that you would love to win. This way you can think about how best to structure your four-year plan to ensure that you will win them.

If you're really motivated, there are college scholarships out there that are specifically offered to high school freshmen, so if you feel a burning desire to compete when most kids are mulling over their current curriculum, go forth and Google.

If you are a sophomore...

There are also scholarships that are available to you, and again, now, before everyone else gets serious, is a great time to apply. At this point you may also want to begin reviewing scholarship applications marketed towards Juniors, since scholarship agencies tend to reuse their questions. Chat with seniors who have won to get a sense of what they were told the scholarship committees were looking for, and possibly recruit one to be your "scholarship buddy" to help you through your own search.

When you run across a scholarship you're interested in pursuing, familiarize yourself with that organization's mission and brand. You should be able to define at least one "ideal" scholarship profile that effectively embodies what the organization is looking for.

If you are a junior...

Sign up for fastweb, scholarships.com, and at least three additional scholarship databases that are specific to your skills, interests, ethnicity or similar factors. Look for scholarships available to students in your grade, then follow the tips in the rest of this book and apply. Meet with your Counselor to discuss all of your options and opportunities you should explore next year. And since your senior year is bound to be very busy, now is also an ideal time to start compiling your list for your big push next year.

If you are a senior...

You're probably in the middle of that big push now, and hopefully following the steps I'm outlining in this book. So keep reading, keep applying, and keep your eyes on the prize. The next few chapters will give you the specific application tips you need to prepare the kind of stellar applications that will win you thousands – and even tens of thousands – in scholarship funds.

Section 4 – Prepare your Package

The organization known as American Atheists offers a Founders' Scholarship, granting money for college to students who are atheist activists in their schools or communities. Applicants must be current college students or high school seniors planning to enter college, have a cumulative GPA of at least 2.5 and have a proven history of involvement in atheist issues – these can include printed letters to the editor, response letters from political leaders on atheist issues, proof that they founded or led an atheist group, testimonials from fellow activists or other clear evidence of their activism. Applicants are also required to submit an essay. Awards are $2,000 for first place and $1,000 for the runner up(s).

Breaking Down the Application

Now comes the moment you've been waiting for – with anticipation, and if you're like a lot of students, possibly a little bit of dread. It's time to fill out your scholarship applications.

What you do now, more than anything else, is going to make or break your chances of winning the scholarship money you want and need to finance your educational dreams. No pressure there, right? But don't worry – like everything else in this book, we'll look at the application process systematically, so you'll feel in

Use pre-printed labels for the envelopes and paper folders that have a business card window in the inside slot. Have some simple business cards printed up with your name, school, and contact information – you can even do them yourself on a computer. Just remember the word *simple* – I'm using it over and over here for a reason. Use one font for your labels and cards, and stick to blue or black ink; you don't want to get too clever. Unless you are going for an art or design scholarship, in which case use your best judgment to guide you.

Since most scholarship agencies make copies of your application for the committee members to review, you don't want to put each page of your application in a single sleeve folder or laminate your application – the idea is to make less work for the people who will be reviewing your application, not more work.

Still, when it comes to presentation, it's the little, cost-free things that matter the most. One scholarship guru I know estimates that nearly 60% of the applications she reviews contain errors. Yes, I said <u>60%</u>. Which is good news for you, because it means that another sure fire way to stand out is simply to make sure *your* applications are error-free. Even if the scholarship application consists of nothing more than a form you fill out online and send in. Please be sure to proofread everything before you hit the "send" button. Remember our tactic for proofreading, (printing and reading the document in 18" font). Ask your Reviewer or another Board member to provide a set of additional eyes to catch any errors you may have overlooked.

If an application form provides a space for an essay, do not, I repeat, *do not* type your essay directly onto the application. You will want to devote plenty of time and attention to your essays, have your Reviewers read them, and revise them to make them as strong as possible. We'll take a more in-depth look at application essay writing later in this chapter – but for now, plan to write all of your essays in your word-processing program and DO NOT copy and paste an essay onto your application form until it's been reviewed, revised and polished to the point where you're confident it is as good as it can possibly be.

Then, just to be safe, check it one more time.

Letters of Recommendation

Most scholarships will ask for letters of recommendation to be included with your application – this is where the Recommenders you've selected for your Board come in. We've already gone over the specifics of what you want from your Recommenders. You should already have your letters, but I'll go over it one more time, just in case.

Remember, you'll want to be as involved as each Recommender will allow you to be in the development of your letters. Make sure your Recommenders know and understand the story you are trying to convey, and make it clear (in the nicest way possible) that you're hoping their letters will be relevant to and supportive of your theme. Give them all the information they need – a brief resume listing your accomplishments complete with facts and figures is an excellent tool. And, as I mentioned before, so are cookies. A little gratitude can get you a lot in life.

That said, every Recommender is different and you may not be able to exert much direct influence over yours. This may not matter – an incredibly private teacher or administrator may write you an amazing letter with very little input from you. Just remember, whether you ultimately want to use a letter of recommendation is up to you. You should already have your letters ready to go well in advance of any scholarship deadlines, so if any letters fail to sing your praises adequately, you will have time to enlist another Recommender. Also, this should go without saying, but review the letters (if the Recommenders permit it) to read their comments, check for typos, and confirm a consistent message is carried across all parts of your application. Just because your Recommenders are professional adults doesn't mean they're perfect.

Your Resume – Awards, Extracurriculars

Generally, scholarships ask for resumes and/or lists of any honors and awards you've received. Your scholarship application will likely have a space where you can attach a resume or list the honors and awards you've won, as well as the extracurriculars and activities you've participated in both in and out of high school. And amazingly, many scholarship applicants respond by supplying...nothing.

Expert Tip

"Many students completely disregard this section and miss great opportunities to distinguish themselves. This part of the application is just as important as the others. So many

students do not use all of the fields, which hurts them, because we award points for each award. Never lie, but never forget to include all of your accomplishments."

On the other hand, you may be tempted to fill that space in simply by adding new entries as you remember them until you run out of space.

Don't do that.

This section of a scholarship application isn't just a data field that needs filling; it's a great opportunity to shine. I included a separate write-up devoted exclusively to this area with my applications – it helped me stand out, and I highly recommend doing it. Instead of just listing the awards I won and the things I did, I provided background and context – and of course, numbers.

Go to www.educationalkeys.com to view the actual resume I submitted along with the scholarships I applied to.

What does that mean? Well, for example, instead of saying you won your school's AP English award, say you won the AP English award, placing first out of a highly competitive class of 125 Junior AP English students. And don't say you won your school's Out-standing Service Award; say you won the Outstanding Service Award for organizing a fund-raising dinner that netted $2,500 to help victims of the Haitian earth-quake.

An online application may not provide you additional space to include a document like mine – in fact, it might not even include enough space to simply list all of your accomplishments (I'm talking about you, Mr. Spectacular). If that's the case, take a moment to think before you type. Consider the organization that's offering the scholarship and what matters to them. When you select the awards and activities to enter, use the ones that relate most directly to their mandate and your story first – unless you've won some particularly prestigious awards. You always should prioritize awards by relevance to your story and the organization you're applying to. Remember, every piece of information you give the scholarship committee contributes to their overall picture of you, so think about the picture you're creating.

Other Stuff

Some applications require some extra materials

beyond the specifics we've discussed here – anything from a PowerPoint presentation to a video to something you've built or designed. It all depends on the type of scholarship/competition you're applying for. Again, the important thing to remember is that regardless of what a particular scholarship committee asks you to submit, whatever you *do* submit is a reflection of you. So make sure you put as much care, quality and individuality as possible into anything you submit – and keep it consistent with your story.

Crafting your Story

That story – the thing we've been talking about throughout this chapter and this book – is the heart of your application. Your goal with each application should be to interweave your story throughout all of the components – the initial form, the awards and activities, the essay, the letters of recommendation – regardless of what "type" of application it is and what material you submit.

This all sounds great, right? But exactly how do you do this?

As a scholarship applicant, you are presenting yourself as a potential investment opportunity. And for a committee to invest its money in You, Inc., they need to understand the underlying value and potential return on that investment. Your story will help scholarship committees see You the way you want to be seen.

Your story should cover what you've done, where you are and where you want to go. By linking what you have done in the past with what you want to do in the future, you can establish instant credibility with the committee – you'll show them that you're *already* on the path to success; you're *already* on the way to achieving your goals, so you're a person worth investing in.

Details also make a story read as real and credible – so wherever it's appropriate, quantify your achievements and experiences. Use numbers to show impact. Use names and real organizations in your story to show who you are.

Still, you can use *a little* poetic license with your story. Think of how you might give your parents a slightly altered account of what happened Saturday night from the one you would tell your best friend – the overall narrative might be essentially the same, but the details may be different. This same technique comes in handy when you apply for a scholarship. You are still *you*, your story is still your story, but it can (and should) be tailored to the specific principles and mission of the organization you're applying to.

This is not meant to be confusing – it just means that the details of your story can change depending on whom you're telling it to. If you're applying for a scholarship from a business group, focus on any parts of your story that involve entrepreneurial endeavors. If it's a charitable organization, focus on the money you've raised or time you've given helping others (with as many quantifiable facts and figures as you can produce). If you're asking Pepsi for scholarship money, don't talk about how much you love Coke!

Okay, maybe that wasn't necessary... but seriously. Be cognizant of what organization you're applying to and what matters to them. Answering that last question effectively – what matters most to *them*? – is your best path to scholarship bliss and parades of messages beginning with, "Congratulations, you won."

To help you focus each of what may be many scholarship applications on the right things, it may help to keep these three keys in mind:

- How can I best articulate my value to this scholarship committee?

- How can I provide them a return on their investment and reduce any uncertainty they might have about my potential for success?

- Why would this committee invest in me?

If you think of your life as a painting, your story is the blend of different paint stokes that, working together, create the whole picture. Those paint strokes represent everything you've done leading up to this very moment, so the more new experiences you sought out and the more you have developed as a student and a leader, the more "colors" you'll have on your palette. But even bad experiences can make good material, so don't be afraid to look at and discuss some of the blemishes on your record. Just remember to present a positive spin on that part of your story – how you learned from it, how you overcame it, how it made you a better human being – in the end.

The next step is to synthesize your material, prioritize what's most important to share with the committee and then build your theme. Your theme is the underlying message that ties all the elements of your story together. For example, if you opened your first lemonade stand at the age of seven and are now operating your own online design firm, your theme might be "entrepreneurship." If you've learned to excel despite difficult circumstances like financial or family trouble, your theme might have a common thread of perseverance and gratitude.

Answering the following questions may help unlock your theme:

- What characteristics make you unique?
- What adjectives would your closest friends use to describe you?
- Are you: a leader, performer, athlete, artist, dramatist, scientist, advocate, entrepreneur, etc.
- What are your strengths, interests, passions, fears?
- What do you most enjoy, find rejuvenating?
- What roles do you fill in school?
- What are your goals?
- How do you spend your free time?

Remember, the right answers are the honest answers. This piece is not about what someone else wants to hear. Ultimately, it's up to you to decide what you want to tell them, and do tell them in a *way* that will fulfill their needs. Find what's special about you – everyone has something, I promise! Figure out how it links to the scholarship organization and build your story around that.

Ideally, every piece of information you send in a scholarship application – the application itself, essays, your letters of recommendation and any other projects or supporting material – will all support your theme and your story. Taken all together, everything should give the scholarship committee a clear idea of what makes you unique, special, and most of all, deserving of their money!

•   •   •

The Essay

Nothing strikes more fear into the hearts of seniors than the dreaded application essay. But it really shouldn't. If you're a great writer, an essay (or essays) puts you in the driver's seat, allowing you to tell your story exactly the way you want it told. You can expand on your theme, highlight your accomplishments, tie all the different elements of your application together, explain any weak points in your story and present yourself in the most compelling way possible – as a person the scholarship committee should seriously consider.

If you're not a strong writer, the essay question still presents a great opportunity. You don't need to be a great writer to show that you have the potential to be a great student, especially if you take the time to explain why writing is not your strength – while pointing out the strengths you *do* have – in your essay. Just follow the tips outlined in this chapter to make sure you tell your story in a coherent and consistent manner. Your Board members can help you with this.

Formatting Tips

Even for strong writers, sticking to a format is crucial – it keeps you from wandering off point and helps you focus on answering the committee's questions as best you can.

Most essays will start with a question posed by the scholarship committee, and in some cases, your first step may be choosing from a group of questions. If you have a choice, pick the one that provides the best opportunity to tell your story. If there is no choice offered, think of how to fit *your* story into *their* question.

Once you have your question, your next step is

to create an outline – break the essay down paragraph by paragraph according to the requested format and/or permitted word count. Outline what points you will address in each paragraph – this keeps you from meandering and gives you an easy structure to fill in with all the facts and information you want the scholarship committee to consider.

The first paragraph will be the introduction – and this is where the difference between good writers and great writers begins. Good writers start their essays by immediately beginning to answer the question. Great writers start their essays with information that's relevant to the question, but is designed to draw the attention of the reader.

What do I mean by this? Well, which essay would you be more interested in reading when asked "what are your career goals?"

> *"My career goal is to become a lawyer. I have always wanted to become a lawyer, since observing my father save lives."*

Or...

> *"Twenty-five lives saved, millions of tears avoided, many life-shaking testimonies heard, and countless expressions of gratitude ex-*

pressed for my father, all because he success-
fully helped clients avoid death row. I, too,
want to become a lawyer to further support
wrongly accused people."

Your goal is not only to answer the essay question in this first paragraph, but to capture the reader's attention – so clearly the second sample did a better job. You'll also want to set up how you will explain your answer in next few paragraphs. However, don't be tempted to wait for a subsequent paragraph to answer the question. Committee members read a lot of essays, and may only read the first few sentences of yours. Then again, they may read the entire thing, so be sure that the points you address in paragraphs two, three and four relate back to what's in paragraph one.

In other words, don't write in your intro, *"My goal is to play college rugby for a Division One school"* and then write a follow-up paragraph about why you love playing the piano. Instead, you might want to address how you got started playing rugby in your first paragraph, move to your accomplishments in the second and talk about your future goals – and how your experiences taught you transferable skills that will help you on the field in college. Keep it organized and easy to follow, and make sure each paragraph relates back to your original theme.

Fleshing Out Your Essay

Remember, regardless of what your essay is about, examples are critical – and by examples, I mean mention the actual names of organizations you belonged to, awards you won, classes you took and excelled in as opposed to simply saying you're "interested in" or "good at" something. Previous performance is a reliable predictor of future performance, so the more concrete your examples, the easier it will be for the scholarship committee to place you on the "Winning" trajectory. Anytime your story is substantiated with quantifiable examples that affirm your statements, you strengthen your point.

Don't dwell on your failures and weaknesses in your essay, but don't avoid them entirely either. Your essay is the ideal place to explain why your grades may have been lower one year, or why you don't have a lot of extracurricular activities. Present them as an opportunity for improvement, as well as proof that you're a real human being. Then follow up with something proactive you're doing or have done to address the problem. For example:

> "My grades suffered during my sophomore year since I was a student athlete, working 25 hours a week, and babysitting my younger siblings. Since education was my top priority, I quit my after-school job, and convinced my coach to implement rules conducive to studying on the hour bus rides home. I now lead group study sessions for my teammates and as team captain, I punish the group anytime someone scores less than 80 on a test by forcing the entire team to run additional miles."

This essay paragraph deals with a problem – low grades – and provides an explanation – work and sports. However, it also shows that the writer is proactive, a leader of his peers *and* someone who is able to influence adults, all in one example. It turns a negative into an even stronger positive.

Throughout your essay, check back to make sure your message is consistent with your theme. Strive for the right balance between enough and too much information – and keep the overall focus positive. Make sure any goals you articulate are reachable. For example, "*I want to become the first Asian-American President by the age of 25*" is not reachable – partly because you have to be 35 to be President. Instead, try something like, *"My long-term goal is to be the first Asian-American President; however, my short-term goal is to volunteer in D.C. for a political party to learn the inner structures of campaign management."*

· · ·

Also remember to find a way to link your experiences and strengths back to the scholarship organization you're applying to. Look for what you have done that embodies their principles and focus on those points. An entrepreneurial organization might not be especially interested in a future rugby star's on-field successes – unless the student can find a way to link what he's learned or accomplished on the field back to the business world, e.g., *"As the team captain, my team looked to me for leadership and direction. I grew comfortable with leading and taking mitigated risks to make us successful."* Know what the scholarship is about and write your essay with that in mind. Even if your accomplishments are not an obvious fit, like Mr. Rugby Stud and the business world, some of his experiences, like leading a team, setting goals and accomplishing them, can be "spun" to better fit the organization's worldview.

Sometimes, crafting a winning essay can be as

simple as taking the time to do a little research.

For example...

Mr. Spectacular wrote an essay detailing why he was great and should therefore be given money.

Ms. Prepared researched the scholarship first and saw that the company's mission was to equip tomorrow's leaders with the resources to be team players. Additionally, Ms. Prepared read on the company's site that scholarship winners are paired with mentors. So Ms. Prepared wrote her essay about a group chemistry project that taught her the importance of working with others. Additionally, she mentioned how she really thinks that a mentor would be instrumental in her college career to help her choose the right courses.

Guess who won that scholarship?

Consistency is Key...

Every essay starts with a purpose and a theme. The purpose of your essay – even if the question is not "Why should we award you our scholarship dollars?" – is actually to persuade the scholarship committee to choose you and award you the money.

The theme of your essay is your story (as it relates to the scholarship organization's mission, of course). So make sure you connect every specific example, every anecdote and every scenario in your essay directly back to your story. All the information you present must be relevant, or directly related, to your journey. This is called "consistency," and it's a huge key to what makes a competitive application successful.

Consistency makes your story appear real and credible. When all of your scholarship materials – your essays, letters of recommendation, and all other application documents – reinforce your story and your theme, things seem to be in harmony, there are no sour notes or off-key elements in your presentation.

Of course, there will be occasions when you are basically asked to write an essay about why you need scholarship money. In that case, don't just write, *"I need money to pay for school, because I don't want my family to take out loans."* Or, *"I need money to pay for school, so I can buy a new car and not have to take the bus."* Regardless of how valid those reasons are, the key is to remember you're playing **Scholarship Taboo**. Specific and valid reasons, including, *"I need money to help pay for school, because I plan to complete a dual major in*

Business and Economics, which will limit the number of hours I can work a campus job," are going to get you much further.

Just saying you don't want loans does not make you seem deserving – no one wants loans! Instead, focus on the reasons you need money: funding for program fees, to attend academic-related trips, reduce the number of hours you would have to work, paying for tutors, books, meal plans, etc.

Remember, wherever possible, quantify and be specific. Applications that stand out contain measurable results with quantifications. For instance, an essay that states, *"I collected coats for the less fortunate"* fails in comparison to one that states, *"During my term as President of YEP organization, I spearheaded a coat drive and collected 300 coats to donate to the less fortunate in the inner-city of Detroit."*

If you're unable to write everything you've done in your essay, find a subtle way to include the information in other areas of the application such as the awards and accolades or extracurricular activities section. If you worked with an organization that isn't widely known, include brief descriptions of the organizations and awards to help the scholarship panel better understand what you've done. Do not assume the agency already knows all about your accomplishments – your completed application is your opportunity to showcase them.

Get Feedback

Once you've completed a draft of a scholarship essay, it's essential that you get feedback. Show it to your reviewers and as many other people (Board members, students who have been there, English teachers, parents) as possible. Don't just look for approval; look for concrete suggestions on how to improve. And most importantly, make sure it is uniquely you as your story should not read as generic as John Doe's story. If anyone else could have signed his or her name on your same essay, your essay is not doing its job. Go back and make it more personal, use more examples from your life, and talk more about what the money will mean to you in terms of pursuing your education and your dreams.

Visit www.educationalkeys.com and sign up to review additional essays that won.

A Few More Tips...

One way to get a clear idea of what scholarship organizations are looking for is to talk with students who have won these scholarships in the past. Ask if you can see their essays and talk with them about their stories and how they constructed their applications.

Some agencies also publish a list of recent scholarship winners, and maybe even those winners' essays. Read whatever you can and learn as much as possible about what made the winners special. If there is contact information included, consider reaching out to them for advice.

Scholarship agencies are embracing social media and using Facebook and Twitter as mediums to reach broad audiences. If you can subscribe to their pages, you may be able to learn valuable information that will help you in the application process.

Blogs are a growing source of unbias information. Read forums and blogs to get additional information. www.educationalkeys.com has a blog section to help students organize information and share stories about their experiences applying for scholarships.

What You Should Be Doing Now

If you are a freshman...

Most of your energy should be spent thinking about the story you want to build, and beginning to put that story together. Have you joined a student organization? Have you begun to play sports, joined the newspaper or won a part in a play? Are you volunteering? It's important to do something constructive with your spare time so you can start building a record of achievement both in and out of the classroom. You should also consider noting down experiences that fit with your theme. For example, accomplishments you made in an organization or team learning experiences you had that edified you. Looking at the kinds of questions those five scholarships you chose from before, take a moment at the end of each semester to consider experiences that you might be able to write about as potential responses to the questions.

If you are a sophomore...

By now, you should be well on your way to building your story – so it's time to make sure you are involved in a variety of activities and excelling in at least some of them. Work on perfecting your essay writing, and get help from a teacher if necessary. To get an idea of what you'll be doing in two years, ask if you can review some of your older peers' applications. You can even write your own practice essays answering the specific questions on those applications. Then ask a teacher or other expert you trust to review your work, and take note of their suggestions.

If you are a junior...

If you're a junior and you haven't done the above yet, now is the time to do it. Talk with your senior friends about the scholarships they are applying for, read their applications and practice tailoring your story to different scholarship applications. The more skill you have adapting your story and your record of accomplishments to different organizations with different mandates, the better off you will be next year when you take on the application process.

If you are a senior...

At this point, you're likely in the middle of it all, so any work you've done in previous years will pay off now. Focus on researching scholarships, identifying previous winners and learning as much as you can about them. Find out how much money each organization gives, if the winners generally all major in a particular subject, and if there are any similarities in their biographies. As for the organizations themselves, Google them, look for recent press releases to see what they're currently focused on, and learn all you can about the people you will be asking for money. The more you know about them, the better you can tailor your story to their interests.

Then you can send out your applications, knowing you've done the very best you can to separate yourself from the crowd, and get ready for the next possible step in the process – the Interview.

Section 5 – Ace Your Interview

Can you quack like a duck? Are you a high school senior in the United States? Then the Chick & Sophie Major Memorial Scholarship Duck Calling Contest may be for you. Contestants must complete four duck calls, according to the rules of the World's Championship Duck Calling Contest, within 90 seconds. The calls are the hail, feed, comeback and mating calls. Prizes include a $2,000 scholarship for the winner, $1,000 for the first runner-up, $750 for the second runner-up and $500 for the third runner-up. Contact the Stuttgart Chamber of Commerce in Stuttgart, Arkansas, to register.

At this point, you may be thinking the hard part of your scholarship search is over. You've filled out your applications and written your essays, so all that's left to do is wait for the (hopefully positive) results, right?

Not exactly.

You may still need to do an interview. Or even several interviews.

Not all scholarship organizations require interviews, and there's no one hard and fast rule to use to determine whether you should expect to do one. However, because their pool of applicants are all in one general area, local scholarship organizations may be more likely to ask for in-person interviews than national scholarship organizations. Additionally, more and more national organizations are adding phone interviews to their application processes. Generally, the larger the award offered, the more likely it is that a scholarship committee will want to meet its potential investment in some fashion.

This hopefully doesn't scare the bejeezus out of you.

If you've never had a part-time or afterschool job, chances are you've never sat down with an adult and been officially "interviewed" before. Actually, even if you've been working for years, sitting down with the assistant manager of your local Golden Arches to discuss the finer points of running the deep fryer is probably a lot less terrifying than meeting with a successful, professional "grown up" who may hold the key to your academic future.

As I've said before, no pressure there...

However, scary as it sounds, an interview with a representative of a scholarship committee can be a very, very good thing. It gives that committee the chance to see the real, genuine human being you really are, and gives *you* an all important opportunity to connect with that scholarship committee on a personal level and show them why you are the person the committee's been looking for.

Read on to find out how.

Scheduling an Interview

If a scholarship organization you've applied to requires or offers an interview, you will probably be notified. The information is usually listed in the application material, including whether the interviews are typically held in person or by phone, and instructions on how to go about scheduling yours.

If the interview is optional, you may be wondering whether you should do it. It might sound like a risk – you put so much effort into your application, and if you say one stupid thing one time, you could ruin everything, right?

Honestly, it's not likely. In the overwhelming majority of cases, sitting for an interview can only improve your chances of winning a scholarship. It proves that you're taking the opportunity seriously, and it gives you a chance to make your case in person – a situation where people are much more easily won over to your cause and more likely to tell you "yes."

Look at the "to interview or not to interview" question as Economics 101 – does the opportunity cost of going outweigh the opportunity cost of not going? Chances are good that the opportunity to promote your brand, to tell your story and to show the scholarship committee what makes you special will far outweigh any risk that you might screw up. If your interviewer has experience, he or she has likely seen dozens of people make mistakes and will take any missteps on your part in stride. If your interviewer is new, he or she may be just as worried about saying the wrong thing.

The bottom line is, *you* shouldn't worry. No one expects you to be perfect during an interview. They only expect you to be you – and this chapter will help you present the best *you* possible during your interviews.

And if you're not really worried about interviewing but think you might skip it anyway? I don't care how busy you are, an optional interview is something you need to make the time for. If you can't attend the interview, work out an alternative – try to schedule it for another day, ask to meet at or near a place where you'll be playing a sport or volunteering, do whatever it takes to show that you are interested in the organization and want to meet, even if it's only for a phone interview. Take the agencies you apply to seriously, and they will take you seriously.

Preparing for the Meeting

Once you've scheduled an interview, your next step is to be sure you walk in with something to say. And by something, I mean more than "I need money." You want to demonstrate that you're a serious person who is interested in more than having the agency's money in your pocket – you're also interested in using that money to pursue something the agency cares about.

This means you need to do your research. Visit the organization's website and familiarize yourself with its mission statement, history and latest news. Make sure you understand why the organization is offering scholarships and what qualities it's looking for recipients to have. Look for areas where its mission and your story overlap – you should already have some idea of this from the application process. Now, however, you need to immerse yourself in the organization and how its mission relates to you to the point where you can sit down and *talk* about it.

Expert Key:

"*Students that win our scholarship know exactly what to communicate. They front-load their answers and lead in with summary action words that show a connection between our mission and their personal story. We have to take notes during the interview, so the easier students make it for us, the more likely we'll capture the essentials of the conversation. For instance, if a leadership-oriented agency asks you for your three greatest strengths, a proper response starts with three action words (front loaded) and incorporates leadership-oriented answers into the examples (mission connection). A great answer would begin, 'My three greatest strengths are my charisma, vision, and self-awareness,' (three qualities of great leaders). 'As the captain of the debate team, my charisma helped... In organizing the senior campaign, my vision set the foundation for... When asked to be class president, my self-awareness of my personal objectives led...' Notice the interviewee mentioned the three adjectives first, ensured his response related to the organization's mission, and provided concise concrete answers."*

Clearly, the "great answerer" mentioned above was ready to talk, and you need to be equally prepared to talk about your own accomplishments, as well as your goals for the future. A good interview is really just an extended conversation, so make sure you arrive at your interviews with some key things you want to discuss in mind. Self-awareness is essential, as is your ability to relay the story you have been telling throughout the application process in person. So know in advance which of your personal areas you want to highlight, including your strengths, weaknesses (and how you've overcome them), goals, vision, collaborative nature, whatever matters most – and ensure all of your responses connect to your theme in relation to the organization's mission. Though interviewers are interested in learning more about you, remember they are interested in learning more about you to determine if you embody their scholarship's purpose.

Some general information you should be ready to

talk about and should think through well in advance of your interview will include:

- Why do you want the scholarship? (No, not because you need the money and/or don't want to take out loans, but because of what those scholarship dollars will enable you to accomplish.)

- Why would this organization want to give you its money over all the other applicants? (An area where knowing something about the organization you're applying to is very helpful!)

- Some questions about the organization you're meeting with – asking about anything, from current events (Google press releases and/or articles on the agency or company's site) to its history, shows you have an interest in the organization. Make sure your questions are POSITIVE.

- Your elevator pitch – we discussed the specifics back in Section 2 – check back on page (49) for a reminder on how to build yours. Make sure you walk into your interview knowing your goals, accomplishments, and current state.

If ever asked about your weaknesses, be sure to

always mention them along with proactive measures you've taken to improve in that area – e.g.,

> *"As a natural leader, my first instinct is to volunteer for leadership positions. This has been a weakness, because I have had to give up a lot of sleep and learn 'under fire.' To mitigate this, I have now taken an observer role in clubs and organizations, and look to volunteer only when I'm 100% confident I have the capacity to take on the project."*

Finally, take some time to practice your interviewing skills – running through the process a few times will make you more comfortable when it's time for the real thing. See if your Counselor is available for some practice sessions, reach out to your Board members, and even try some of your parents' friends. You want to replicate the real interview feeling as much as possible; so if your interview will be in Starbucks, ask a Board member to meet you at Starbucks for a session. The idea is to get as comfortable as you possibly can talking about yourself with adults, answering their questions and holding up your end of a conversation – which also means listening to what the other person has to say and responding thoughtfully. Remember, this is not a speech, it's an interview.

Of course you can always hold mock interviews with your friends, but remember that in real life, you probably won't know your interviewer and the dynamics between the two of you will be a lot more formal. So try to maintain a level of professionalism with your friends. You can always make fun of each other when you've finished practicing.

And if you do well, you can laugh all the way to the bank.

It can also be extremely helpful to see yourself and identify and understand some of your own idiosyncrasies. One way to witness those idiosyncrasies in action is to record yourself answering some of the interview questions above with your camera, iPad, cell phone, or any other recording device. Afterwards, review your practice interview. You should be able to spot where you could have added more information, or might have achieved more by saying less. Even more importantly, you can pick out any bad habits like saying "um" or "you know" too much, or not looking up, or laughing nervously. Sometimes we have no idea how we actually come across to others, so being able to see yourself will provide some needed clarity on how you can improve.

If Your Interview Will Be Over the Phone...

An increasing number of organizations are using phone screens or phone interviews – it lowers their costs while making it much easier to interview large volumes of people.

If your interview will be held over the phone, do some housekeeping beforehand. Clean up your voice-mail and make sure your outgoing message is clear and professional. Since no one will actually see you talking, you can have notes with bullet points prepared, so you'll be able to keep track of exactly what points you want to make. When the actual interview happens, take the call standing up – your voice will project better and you'll sound more confident. You'll also want to be within reach of a computer with internet access if possible – maybe with the organization's website up on your screen for easy access.

Expert Tip:

From a large, national organization that inter-

views hundreds of candidates...

"Interview candidates that perform very well front-load their answers with action words that can easily be written down. This is beneficial to the candidate because the interview form generally involves a sliding scale with a comment box. E.g. "Did the candidate effectively articulate both short-term and long-term goals?" The scale has Poor, Fair, Good, Very Good and Excellent.

Therefore, if asked what are three adjectives that describe you, state the three adjectives first, elaborate on the why you chose each adjective and remain conscious that your interviewer is completing a form that he or she must submit with notes. Some interviewers are able to remember your conversations verbatim, but the overwhelming majority will benefit from having you include transition words to guide them and their notes. Additionally, leading the conversation with strong buzz words will only improve the interview for both parties."

The Big Day

Getting ready for your interview can be more nerve-wracking than getting ready for the prom, so just take it one step at a time. You want to be clean and comfortable, so shower if at all possible, wear deodorant, brush your teeth, make sure your hair is as neat and professional-looking as it gets.

What should you wear? That depends on where your interview will take place. If you'll be meeting at an office, formal business attire is your best bet – a conservative blue or grey suit for men with a simple tie and shirt, preferably white or blue. The equivalent applies for women – pants or a skirt, your choice. The idea here is not to make a major style statement; you'll be showing your personality in other ways so, if anything, you don't want your clothes competing for attention.

An off-site interview, say at a Starbucks or somewhere like that, can be a little trickier. Chances are, if you speak with your interviewer beforehand, he or she will let you know if the dress code is casual. If they don't, you may want to check the organization's website or even call and ask – better to be safe than sorry. And if you are told casual dress is fine, no, this does not mean wear your board shorts and a T-shirt with a clever phrase on it. Think "business casual" – a polo shirt and khakis for men, or a nice top and skirt or pants for women, means you won't feel underdressed and out of place.

And whatever you wear, once you put it on, don't eat anything and only drink very carefully! If you know you have to eat beforehand, you may want to avoid messy food or bring along a change of clothes, just in case.

Don't walk into your interview empty-handed – the interviewer may have a file with your information, but the easier you make it for him or her, the more complete and seamless your presentation, the better you'll come across. Bring a portfolio binder with a notebook, pen, and copies of your resume, along with your essays. You can also bring some notes to use during the interview – you are certainly not required to memorize everything, and a bulleted page of items you want to cover or discuss is perfectly acceptable. Write out at least two thoughtful questions you might have for the organization a few days before the real interview to make sure you have something prepared to say, and jot down some notes covering what you want to highlight about you.

Even if you're confident that you can handle the entire interview off the cuff – and if you can, you absolutely should, as this is sure to impress your interviewer – bring your notes with you in case your brain crashes and burns under pressure. Having a back-up plan in the midst of disaster may look even more impressive by showing your interviewer how serious and thorough you are.

Finally, make sure to leave early enough that you'll arrive about 15 minutes before your interview is scheduled so you can visit the bathroom and touch up your makeup, hair or clothes, and most importantly, take a minute to relax. Long deep breaths will help, as will reminding yourself that your interviewer is only human and is probably not expecting perfection. Turn your cell phone off or set it to silent. You don't even want your phone vibrating during your interview. You want the interviewer to feel that he or she has your full and complete attention.

During the Interview

When you meet your interviewer, smile, look him

or her in the eye and shake hands. For a calm, confident handshake, remember "web to web" – inside of the "web" between your thumb and forefinger should connect with the same spot on your interviewer's hand. If you're nervous, you can admit it – your interviewer will probably expect it, and it will humanize you. However, becoming a quivering heap will not send the right message, so no matter how nervous you are, remember to keep it together. The right body language will convey the right message – that you're confident in who you are and ready to talk about yourself.

Scholarship interviews generally last at least 30 minutes, allowing enough time for a fairly in-depth conversation. Expect your interviewer to take the lead – he or she will likely come to the interview with a list of specific questions already prepared for you to answer. At the same time, you should be ready to gently guide the conversation to your theme and the list of bullet points you've prepared. Listen for key words in the conversation that relate to your story or your goals, and don't be afraid to take control of the discussion at those instances and elaborate.

However, remember, again, that you're not making a campaign speech. Allow the conversation to "breathe," and make sure your interviewer can get a word in edgewise. After all, you're there so your interviewer can ask you questions his or her organization wants answered – so make sure you allow that to happen. These questions will probably include:

- Tell me about yourself.

- What are your goals?

- What are you passionate about?

- How can our organization help you achieve those goals?

As for the questions you should ask, now is the time to subtly show that you've done your research. Add in relevant information that you've picked up from the organization's website or press coverage – try to move beyond those questions that are easily answered via a company's website (as in, "When was your organization established?") and try to focus on something open-ended that can spark a discussion (e.g., "Despite the turbulent economy, I notice you gave out a record number of scholarships last year. To what do you contribute your organization's success?"). And if you can find a way to discuss something about *their* organization that relates to *your* story, well, that's basically a home run.

Some interviews fly by so fast and cover so much you won't even know where the time went. Others... maybe not so much. Sometimes there are lulls in the conversation, and if there is in yours, remember not to panic and try to fill in the silence with a lot of jabbering. Silence is perfectly acceptable – it gives interviewers time to take notes, to think, to formulate the next question. If things really, really seem stalled, use the moment to ask questions or elaborate on parts of your story. Remember, just because your interviewer is sitting across from you, that doesn't necessarily mean he or she is a "great talker." Your interviewer is also only human, and your understanding of that fact will make the process easier for both of you.

Sometimes wondering when and how to end an interview can be stressful. Generally, your interviewer will take the lead on this; however, keep an answer to this question – "If the meeting has to end in five minutes, what's the one thing I really want the interviewer to know about me?" – in your mind. If you haven't shared that piece of information, and the interview seems to be winding down, work it into the conversation.

If it looks like time is running out, or if you're simply out of questions, you can tell your interviewer, "Those are the only questions I have prepared," then ask for his or her contact information, "in case anything else comes to mind." Make sure you thank the interviewer for meeting with you, shake his or her hand, look him or her in the eye, and ask what the next steps are.

Then, once the interviewer is safely out of sight, you can congratulate yourself on a job well done.

Follow-up

Some people send thank you emails as a kind gesture after an interview is over, but many others don't. It's really up to you – if it feels right, do it, but if you'll toss and turn at night thinking, "Why did I do that?" then by all means, don't. Don't overthink it.

Just remember, even an interview that doesn't go perfectly or doesn't end up bringing you the results you were hoping for is still a good thing. At some point in your life, you are bound to go through several more interviews with adults in positions of authority who have been called upon to evaluate you. Every interview is a learning experience, every interview makes you stronger, every interview means you will be better the next time. Therefore, every interview is worthwhile.

What You Should Be Doing Now

If you are a freshman...

Again, you should primarily be focused on laying the groundwork for a stellar high school career, building your story, and figuring out what you're good at and what you enjoy. Of course, if this is the path you're planning to walk, it's never too early to develop your interviewing technique; so just try to stay open to conversations and don't hide away from adults. Instead, practice talking to the "grown-ups" you know so you can develop a comfort level that will be there down the line.

If you are a sophomore...

At this point, you should definitely be starting to hone your "adult conversation" techniques. Make sure you're getting out in the world and talking with a variety of people. Don't isolate yourself in a world exclusively populated by other teenagers. Get a sense of what's going on in the real world! Now may also be an ideal time to join organizations that offer exclusive scholarships for their members.

If you are a junior...

Now is the time to talk with your senior friends about their interviews – you can even start practicing with the adults you know, or your friends. At this point, you should also be stepping up in student organizations, taking an active role around campus, and hopefully talking and interacting with the adults involved. Some of those adults will likely become part of your Board of Directors, so recruiting them for those positions can give you something to talk about.

If you are a senior...

As a senior, you will likely be starting your interviews very soon. Make sure you've nailed your elevator pitch and practice it so that you can deliver it under just about any circumstance. Go over interview techniques with Board members, practice with whoever has time for you, and remember to do your research on each organization you meet with *before* the interview. Be sure to have well thought out questions that shows you know about the organization and will give back.

Follow the steps in this chapter (and the previous chapters), and you should have no trouble showing scholarship committee members who you are, what you're all about, and why you deserve their money and help. So in the next chapter, we'll take a look at what you should do when that money starts rolling in.

Section 6 – Manage your Money

If you're a tall teen -- a male over 6'2" or a female over 5'10", Tall Clubs International just might help you pay for your education. Every year at their annual convention, TCI awards scholarships of up to $1,000 each to soon-to-be freshman students. To qualify, you must be under 21, planning to enter your first year of college and, most importantly, you must be sponsored by the TCI member club closest to you. To learn more, visit the organization's website at www.tall.org.

Your applications are in. Your interviews are done. At this point, there's really only one thing left to do.

Wait.

Which, to some of us, is actually the hardest part of the whole scholarship application experience.

I don't have to tell you that waiting sucks. Obviously, if you knew in advance that you were going to win every single scholarship you applied for, you could go on with your life and survive the next few weeks or months without giving your applications a second thought. But the reality is that it's not that easy. Chances are, some of the organizations that you applied to are going to say no.

Yes, that even applies to you, Mr. Spectacular. But I promise, it's not the end of the world.

Beating the Odds

There's one sure way to increase the probability that you will win all the scholarship money you need to finance the education you want. Apply to a whole lot of them. I, personally, applied to 72 scholarships.

And I graduated from Cornell University, a school with a sticker price above 50 grand a year, with exactly zero dollars of debt.

So while 72 applications might sound excessive, or even obsessive, to some of you, what that indicates to me is that for me, 72 was the right number of scholarships to apply for.

It's not because I won all 72 scholarships. In fact, I'm pretty sure I lost most of them. I received my share of those responses that kicked me in the gut. But I kept my cool. I looked at each response as an opportunity to learn, and eventually went on to win nearly $500,000 of scholarships – financing an absolute best of the best education without burdening my parents or my future self.

You can do it too – the key is applying to as many scholarships, and as wide a variety of scholarships (that still apply to your skills and talents, obviously), as you possibly can. Cast a wide net – national and local, businesses and interest groups, academic and non-academic – whatever you can find that applies to you. And keep finding new ones to apply to until you've secured all the money you need. It doesn't have to eat up all of your time, especially if you keep all of your material on file and recycle your essays and other application materials where it's appropriate.

Of course, the key word here is "appropriate." While I applied to 72 scholarships and recycled a lot of essays, I remembered the golden rules: "quality over quantity" and "match effort with reward."

Expert Tip:

"After reading essays for seven years, it's obvious when people cut and paste essays from other applications into our fields. Students can leverage other material, but must remain diligent in reviewing the newly crafted essay to make sure it answers the question and flows. Resist temptation to just apply to 1,000 scholarships for the sake of applying. Each application you sub-

mit should accurately represent the best you. Completely fill in scholarship forms, stick to the word count, and give enough attention to each application. If a $500 scholarship requires you to read a 500-page book and write a 3,000-word essay, be mindful of the time you exert applying to that scholarship. Seventy percent of the people who begin applying to our scholarship do not finish their application by the deadline and we award each winner $20,000. Time management is critical and students need not overexert themselves."

Surviving Rejection

It stands to reason that the more you apply, the more rejections you'll receive – and yes, Mr. Spectacular, that includes you. My advice here is, don't cry over them, *use them.*

Most scholarship agencies will email, call, or send a letter informing you of the fate of your scholarship application – pro or con. If the conversation or message begins with, "Congratulations," go ahead and jump up and down – you're a winner! But keep reading, because if you applied to more than one scholarship, I'm pretty sure my next piece of advice will eventually apply to you.

If the message starts with something like, "This year we received an overwhelming response," then yes, that probably means you didn't win that particular scholarship. No doubt this can be discouraging, especially if you feel like you're getting a lot of rejections. But there's a silver lining to the rejection cloud. Those rejections can be the key to crafting better – and even winning – applications.

The key is to approach rejection proactively. When you receive a notification that you did not win a scholarship, wait a week, then contact the committee and politely ask if there's someone there you can talk with briefly about your application. The goal here is not to call up crying or sounding angry and bitter – or anything other than friendly and professional. You're not calling to change their minds, but to pick their brains.

If you've built a personal relationship with someone on the committee, that's an ideal person to reach out to. Send that person an email saying something like,

> *"I applied for your organization's scholarship and unfortunately was not selected as a winner. Given the sheer number of applications you receive, I understand not everyone can be selected. I, however, have another 100 ap-*

plications to fill out and was hoping you or someone from your committee could provide me some feedback on where I can improve my applications. If you're available for a short chat, I can call you anytime that's convenient for you. Thanks in advance for any consideration given this email as your feedback will be instrumental in helping me strengthen my candidacy."

Or something like that.

If the person agrees to talk with you, or if you're directed to someone else, keep the conversation brief (15 minutes or less), have questions prepared, listen to what the person has to say without challenging it (remember, you're not calling to ask that your application be reconsidered or to make someone feel guilty!) and be sure to say, "Thank you for your time and help." Who knows? If the same scholarship is available to current college students, you may be able to apply again and win next year.

Aim to follow up like this with every scholarship you interviewed for – getting an expert take on where you might be able to do better next time will give you invaluable inside knowledge that can only help you improve your applications. The key, really, is to stay strong, stay focused, and never give up.

Before we move on to the fun section of this chapter – what to do with all that money you're going to win – I want to say one last thing about rejection. It can hurt, and it can even cause you to question yourself and your abilities.

You shouldn't.

Honestly, that's not how the scholarship "game" works. Most people receive more rejections than acceptances, so if you do, there's no reason to feel bad about it or take it personally. It's kind of like the game of baseball. If you're a fan, you probably already know that a hitter is considered "great" if he has an average of .300 or more. Which means that the very best hitters – guys who set records, guys who make millions of dollars, guys who are in the Hall of Fame – screw up seven out of every ten times! The lesson here is not to worry about the scholarships you don't get. Focus on the *next* time – keep refining your applications, keep getting advice from your Board, and most of all, keep applying – and soon it will be time to focus on the scholarships you win.

The Thrill of Victory

Obviously, when you get that "Congratulations"

email, letter or phone call, you're going to want to celebrate. So by all means, take a moment to breathe in the victory. Brag a little on Facebook and Twitter. Tell your Mom and Dad.

But don't get too cocky. You still have work to do.

First of all, if you have even one more scholarship to apply to, one of the best moves you can make is to figure out exactly what it was about your application that convinced the committee to award you big piles of cash. The key is to find out while simultaneously strengthening your relationships with the Committee and showing them what a gracious winner (and Future World Beater) you are.

Drop your contact(s) on the Committee an email thanking them for recognizing you – but don't stop there. Ask for an opportunity to learn what aspects of your application helped you land their cash. It might sound complicated, so here's an example you can use...

> *"Thank you for awarding me your (Name) scholarship. It's an honor to be selected amongst the large volume of qualified applicants you received, and I am deeply grateful.*
>
> *I still have several scholarships to apply for in order to fully finance my education, and*

it would be tremendously helpful if I could speak to someone on the committee about the application I submitted. Your agency's feedback would be instrumental in helping me to strengthen my application and hone in on the key attributes that make me a strong candidate.

If you're available for a short chat, I can call you anytime that's convenient for you. Thanks in advance for any consideration given this email, and thank you again for selecting me for your organization's scholarship."

See – gratitude, networking *and* future planning – all in one email. That's the mark of a winner.

Money Matters

Now that you have it, how exactly are you supposed to handle all that money? Chances are you've never won a large amount of money before, and you might be wondering exactly how any scholarship dollars you win are going to get from the organization, to you, and then to a place where you can apply them against your various college expenses. The answer will differ depending on the policies of the school you will be attending and the policies of the organizations awarding you money. However, your goal at this point should be to be as directly involved, and have as much control of your money, as you possibly can.

This starts by asking the scholarship agency, "How does your organization award the money?" Ask if the check will come in a lump sum or in installments, and if in installments, when and for how much.

Also ask if the scholarship will be written directly to you, to your school, or to both? If possible, you want to have the scholarship written directly to you as this will give you full control of the funds. You can then apply the money where you need it most, instead of simply accepting how an organization decides it should be spent. You can even use scholarship money to return home for the holidays or to purchase a new MacBook – whatever you need that generally constitutes a "hidden cost" of college.

To accomplish this, you may need to politely ask the organization to write the scholarship out directly to you, explaining that this will give you more flexibility and assurance that your scholarship will be applied against some of your college expenses. Note the word "politely." Don't be too pushy, since not every organization is going to agree; but for every organization that does, you receive an opportunity you won't want to waste. Ask the organization to mail the scholarship directly to you, if possible, as this will keep you in control.

Sometimes, however, it's just not possible to gain that control. Some scholarship organizations will insist on writing your scholarship directly to your institution, giving the school control over "your" money. If that happens, don't panic. With the right guidance, you'll still be able to exercise the amount of control you need over how the school allocates your money. If this is the case, it doesn't hurt to ask the scholarship agency to mail the checks directly to you, even if those checks are written out to the school. Holding the money gives you some measure of control from the beginning.

Your Financial Aid Counselor

By this point, you should have an idea of what school you'll be attending, how much (if any) aid the school is offering you, and if you'll be participating in a work-study program. Once you've chosen a school, before you even arrive on campus, you'll want to contact the Financial Aid Office and set up a meeting with your Financial Aid Counselor.

When a college awards you a financial aid package (which usually includes grants, work study and loans) you will also receive an estimated total budget, made up of those three components, that represents the total cost you're expected to pay for a semester or a year of school. Keep in mind that a lot of these "total" budgets leave out "hidden" college costs like books, bus passes, laptops, class fees, clothes and travel between home and school – but we'll get to that later.

Your relationship with your Financial Aid Counselor may be the most important relationship in your life during your college years (sorry, Mom). For starters, he or she will help you understand how that combination of loans, grants, and work study fits together and how to apply your scholarship money in the way that does the most for you. To get the most out of your scholarship dollars, ask your counselor to make sure any outside awards you win are first applied to reducing your loans, and then your work study, and lastly to any grants you are entitled to. If you don't, it can cost you a lot of money in the long run. For example:

Mr. Spectacular currently has $10,000 of debt and $20,000 in grants to cover each semester at Smartypants University. He won $15,000 worth of scholarships (for being so darn spectacular, no doubt), and all of them were mailed to S.U. during the first semester. S.U. automatically applied the money to Mr. S's first semester fees, covering his entire $10,000 debt, but also reducing his $20,000 aid package by $5,000. So while this semester will be covered, next semester, Mr. S will have another $10,000 of debt, another $20,000 of grants, but $0 worth of scholarships as all the money will have been spent.

Oops.

Ms. Prepared will also be attending Smartypants U. – and like Mr. Spectacular, has $10,000 in debt, $20,000 in grants and has earned a $15,000 scholarship. Since she met with her Counselor to discuss the school's policies, she knew to call the scholarship organization ahead of time and ask the committee to defer the "extra" $5,000 from her scholarship until her second semester. That way, Smartypants U. receives $10,000 of scholarship money to cover Ms. P's entire debt for the first semester, reducing the amount she owes to $0. And during the second semester, the remaining $5,000 in scholarship money will be applied, reducing Ms. P's $10,000 debt by half and saving her $5,000.

Which is why it pays to be (Ms.) Prepared.

The bottom line is, do the research. Make sure you understand the policies of your institution as well as the scholarship organizations that award you money. You may have to defer scholarships for a semester or a year to make sure the money goes where you want it to go. Be sure to declare any scholarships that have been written directly to you. Your school should be aware of those scholarships, but you should ensure the scholarships work for you.

But remember, your financial aid counselor can do more for you than just make sure your scholarship money goes to the right place.

Expert Tip:

This piece of advice comes from a Financial Aid Counselor who has asked – for obvious reasons – to remain anonymous...

> *"Schools generally have additional aid that we're able to award out that we keep in a reserve account. My colleagues sometimes get angry with me, but I don't mind giving that aid to a student that I've connected with as I sometimes feel financially obligated to help."*

Imagine that student is *you*. Then it's not hard to understand why you want to have a good, strong relationship with your Financial Aid Counselor. Your school may have more money to offer you than stated on your initial award letter. If you're not satisfied with your package, be sure to reach out to your Counselor with a smile and a batch of your by-now-famous freshly baked cookies, because it's going to take more than, "I want more money" to put that cash in your pocket. If you're not confident bringing it up, use the tips mentioned in the interviewing section to help you communicate your needs effectively.

Your situation may also change from year to year, so you'll want to maintain your relationship with your Counselor. For starters, you'll need to complete a new FAFSA every year, and your college will review it and may make adjustments to your aid package based on the results. Don't worry, most packages do not change dramatically year to year. Just remember to keep your scholarships in your back pocket and use them to pay down loans first. Once your loans are paid off, you can defer your outside scholarships until the next semester or year, or you can apply for a budget increase. Sometimes you can get a budget increase to cover those "hidden" costs like trips home for the holidays, or that new MacBook. Keep in mind that these increases usually come in the form of new loans, so if you've paid all of your loans with scholarship funds and still have some left, that additional scholarship money can be applied against the new loan money.

You may also have to request a budget increase to get additional loans in your overall package before having a scholarship organization send in their check. Again, your Counselor will help you understand your school's policies and terms, as well as how to get the most out of your scholarships throughout your college experience. Having a good rapport with your Counselor and understanding your school's financial parameters are the insider's keys you need to be successful.

Key Things to Remember...

1. Don't let rejections get to you – or go to waste. Contact as many organizations as you can and try to learn from your mistakes.

2. Continue to apply for as long as you can, or until you no longer need any more scholarships. There are so many scholarships out there you will not

run out of things to apply for!

3. Recycle your essays wisely. If you reuse an essay or even parts of an essay on another application, be sure it reads as a beautifully crafted essay that reflects your best work. Do not have your essay appear as pieced together as Frankenstein.

4. When you win a scholarship, contact the committee to thank them, and to request a brief discussion of what they liked about your application.

5. Ask the scholarship committee how the money will be distributed, and ask if it can be awarded in your name and to you directly.

6. Meet with your school's Counselor to discuss your funding and any policies the school might have about using scholarship dollars. If you need to defer some scholarship payments, contact your organization and make sure you do so.

7. Maintain your relationships with everyone you meet during the scholarship process – you never know when they might be able help you again, or when you might be able to pay it forward and help someone else.

Section 7 – Money Maintenance

The greeting card company The Gallery Collection offers a $10,000 scholarship to the winner of its annual Create-A-Greeting-Card Scholarship Contest – and also awards $1,000 to the winner's school. Budding graphic artists are invited to submit a photo, computer graphic or piece of artwork to be used on the front of a greeting card, and the designer of the card judged the best takes home the cash. The card can be a Holiday, Christmas, Birthday or "all-occasion" card; however all four previous winners have a Christmas/holiday theme. Only one entry is allowed per person. For more information, go to http://www.gallerycollection.com/greeting-cards-scholarship.htm.

In the last chapter, I attempted to explain everything you need to know about working with the scholarship money you bring in – how to get it in your possession, or at least under your control, to make sure you get the very most out of it over the course of your undergraduate years.

However, staying fully and comfortably financed for your entire college career may take a little more day-to-day effort on your part. You may be flush with funding when you first step on campus as a freshman, but as the years go by, that money will continue to flow out – to the point where you may decide you seriously need to get some more flowing in.

This chapter will help you keep the spigot open. Provided you know what a spigot is.

What is Work Study?

As I mentioned in the previous section, you may have received "work study" as part of your finance package from your college's Financial Aid office. Work study basically means your school will help you get a part-time, most likely on-campus job, and the money you make will cover part of your "expected financial contribution" to your college expenses. The best news is, these jobs are usually much more pleasant than working at the Mickey D's in town, and may even pay more.

Work study comes via the Federal Work Study Program (also conveniently known as FWS), one of the U.S. Government programs that you'll be eligible for after filling out your FAFSA and getting your SAR (Student Aid Report...you have been paying attention, right?). More than 3,000 colleges across the country participate in the FWS program, so chances are good your school will be one of them.

This is another instance where your Financial Aid Counselor will be an invaluable resource. He or she may have quite a bit of power to determine how much FWS money you get, so if I didn't make this clear in the previous chapter, bake some of your renowned cookies and bring them by the Financial Aid Office. Whether you didn't receive work study as part of your package or need additional work study dollars, don't be shy about letting your Counselor know and asking for help.

Get a Job (ya hippie)

If work study is not a part of your financial aid package, don't worry – you can still enjoy the many perks of an on-campus job. Working on your own won't affect your SAR, your job will likely be part-time, and it's not like you'll be making Donald Trump money.

Just be warned, those coveted on-campus jobs may be harder to land at schools where there are a lot of FWS students. But keep looking around – students are always coming and going, so new jobs will open up all the time, and schools need student workers in all kinds of jobs: at the library, in the computer lab, in food service or even helping professors. So even if your "dream job" in the school travel office with the 20% discount on airline tickets isn't available, there very well may be something for you in the campus café.

If you have a few choices in on-campus job, you can stretch your money (FSW or wages) farther by using strategy when you consider where you want to work. The more options available, the better you can tailor what you do to make money to meet your other needs. For example, if you're looking for cheap meals, work in a food service job where you might receive free food, or at least a discount on your meal plan. If you need a place to chill, you can't beat earning a buck in the peace and quiet of the library – and as a bonus, you may be able to study on the job. One of the most coveted campus jobs is the R.A., or Resident Assistant – R.A.s supervise students in their residence halls in exchange for *free room and board*. You can't beat that. But you can even do something as simple as working at a gym to get opportunities to pump iron for free. Whatever matters to you, whatever you need, chances are there's a job that will help you make it happen.

Working for a professor can also be an ideal part-time job – and a key to a whole other world. Developing relationships with faculty members is the next step in your "networking" process anyway – part of college means building relationships with adults, with experts, with people in your field of study, whom you will eventually want to add to your Board and stay in touch with for decades, hopefully. So having a job that puts you face to face with a faculty member you admire can be a very powerful and enriching experience – and still keep the cash flowing.

The bottom line – make smart, targeted choices, approach your on-campus job search with the same focus and creativity you used in your scholarship search, and your part-time job could end up being one of the most valuable aspects of your college experience.

Or you might just get a lot of free food.

Scholarships for College Students

Of course, since this is a scholarship book, I saved the best for last. The best, easiest way to pay your way through college is to continue to apply for – and win – scholarship money throughout your college career. In fact, the very fact that you're in college, studying subjects you care about, pursuing an eventual career, opens up a whole new world of scholarships that probably weren't available to you back in high school.

Remember those millions of scholarship dollars that are available to high school students that I told you about when we started this book? Well, there are also millions of dollars available to current college students. And yes, for the most part, a totally different set of dollars.

Undergraduate scholarships tend to be more focused on specific fields, industries, etc., instead of achievement, interests or talents – so it helps to have some idea of where you fit in and where you're headed. Clearly, if you're an English major who needs a calculator to figure out the tip at a restaurant, you're not going to be pursuing a scholarship designed to help you further your studies in advanced mathematics. However, there are countless scholarships available in every industry, every field for just about every major. Keep this in mind when you Google undergraduate scholarships – use defined key words related to your field of study, like "Undergraduate Scholarships for Engineers" or "Sophomore Art Scholarships."

There's money out there for everything, literally – and as you might expect, large organizations and foundations like Microsoft, JPMorgan, Harry S. Truman and countless other companies and philanthropies, offer hefty scholarships to current college students. Even students interested in completing a semester abroad can find scholarships to help them pay the bills, including the Benjamin A. Gilman International Awards, the CIEE Scholarship, and thousands of others.

Your college may also offer its own scholarships for enrolled students, or may be affiliated with alumni or organizations who offer them specifically at their school or in their area. Again, this will no doubt bring you back to the halls of your Financial Aid office (after you bake yet another batch of those cookies) and another meeting with your Financial Aid Counselor. He or she is bound to know where additional funds are available to enrolled students, and how you can apply for the money.

In fact, colleges and universities across the country have programs and offerings in place to help you pay for college. Your relationship with your Counselor is the key to unlocking all of these. Be open and honest about your needs, and ask if there are any fellowships or school-specific programs designed to help current college students or if there are any other sources of funding out there that you can and should be pursuing.

Finally, even if you wind up with some debt on

graduation day, you still have a few options besides paying it off over time. Companies – specifically the financial companies – and public service organizations like Teach for Americas offer graduates debt forgiveness programs.

As with everything, the key is to approach your finances with open eyes and, even if you're shy, an open mouth. Suffering or worrying in silence will get you nowhere. Asking questions, building relationships and being pro-active won't only get you the money you need – it will also help you lay the foundation for a successful, productive adult life.

Key Things to Remember...

- Stay on top of your financial needs throughout your college career. Very few students walk in with enough scholarship money to cover an entire undergraduate education, but there are ways to supplement your funds while you are in school.

- A work-study job can be more than a way to avoid debt. Selected carefully, it can provide perks from free housing to long-lasting friendships. Think about your priorities and apply accordingly.

- You can work at an on- or off-campus job without seriously affecting your aid package, so if you want to work for pocket money, feel free.

- There are many, many scholarships available to current college students. Apply the same principles you've learned throughout this book, and you should be well positioned to win your share of those millions of dollars.

- Maintain your relationship with your Financial Aid Counselor – he or she will help connect you with any scholarships or other financial programs your school may offer for enrolled students.

What Have We Learned?

At this point, you should know pretty much everything you need to know about finding, applying for and winning your share of the millions of dollars in college scholarship money available to students every year. You've likely picked up some extra information that should help keep you fully financed – and on top of those finances – for the duration of your education. And hopefully, you now feel confident that whatever your family's financial situation might be, whatever the pundits on TV and in the newspaper might say about college costs, a top-level education is not beyond your reach. Provided you meet the requirements for admission, there are things you can do right now and for years to come that should enable you to earn your degree from the school of your dreams.

So let's recap.

First off, you can and should be working to establish yourself as a strong candidate to win scholarship money. You're probably already doing things like exhibiting leadership, achieving academic excellence and excelling in those things you are good at and enjoy – they're the same kinds of activities that will help you get into college in the first place. Now is also the time to start looking for the common themes in your life and creating the "story" of who you are and who you hope to become.

You'll need people in your corner to help you conduct the most effective scholarship search possible – and that's where your "Board" of experts comes in. If you're shy or have trouble talking to adults, it's time to break out of your shell (and break out the homemade cookies), so you can begin to approach some people you like and trust and ask for their help. Ideally, you'll want to recruit an Advisor, typically a favorite teacher or other adult, to help oversee your scholarship search and provide advice, encouragement and the occasional kick in the butt (if you need it).

You'll want to forge the strongest relationship possible with your high school Counselor, as he or she is your link to all of the services your high school provides when it comes to scholarships. Look for the best

Recommenders – reliable people who know and respect you, and have the skills and time to convey that – to write letters that will effectively sing your praises and reinforce your story. Finally, enlist a skilled and tough Reviewer or two to make sure your applications and essays are the best they can be.

When it comes to finding funding for your education, you'll start by filling out the FAFSA, which not only determines your eligibility for government assistance, but also helps colleges – many of which have endowments to help students pay for their education – determine the amount of financial aid to award you.

Next, you'll move into your scholarship search. Make sure you've organized a system where you can save all of the information you've uncovered so you can easily access it and keep track of what you've done. Since there are thousands and thousands of scholarships out there, devise a search system that works for you, starting at your high school – which may offer scholarships or links to local organizations that offer them – and moving out into your local community. Your state may offer specific scholarships, and so might the college you've been admitted to. Finally, there are thousands of national and international scholarship organizations that offer money to deserving students. Look for organizations that relate to your interests and skills for the best odds of winning.

When you start applying for scholarships, remember to take time to fill out each application neatly and correctly – 60% of students don't, so this will give you an automatic leg up. Refine your story to spotlight what makes you special and unique and tailor it to each specific scholarship you're applying to, highlighting the things you have in common with the organization's mission. If possible, attach a separate resume of your honors and achievements – if not, and especially if space is limited, remember your overall story and think about the organization before you decide what items to enter onto your application form. Make sure your letters of recommendation reinforce your story. And follow simple guidelines to write a strong essay, even if you're not a strong writer, that will help scholarship members feel a connection to you, your story and your future.

If you have the opportunity to sit down with a scholarship committee member for an interview, consider yourself lucky and do it! A face-to-face meeting can likely only help you in your quest to win a scholarship. Memorize your elevator pitch and a few key points about your experience, interests and goals. Practice in advance with a friend or, even better, your Advisor. Don't forget to dress appropriately for where the interview will take place. And most of all, relax. Your interviewer is only human and will forgive any small mistakes you make. You can even bring notes with you if you're worried you might leave something out.

Once you start winning scholarship money, make sure it goes as far as possible. Try to get the money awarded to you, in your name. Even if you can't manage that, you'll want to have a relationship with your college's Financial Aid Counselor. He or she will help you make sure any aid you receive from the government or the school is allocated to expenses first, so the scholarship money you win goes as far as it possibly can. If you need extra help, your Financial Aid Counselor can help you with a work-study job or loans to make sure the money keeps flowing in. And you can continue to use the tips in this book to apply for more scholarships to finance you through your undergraduate years – and beyond.

Will it all be easy? Just as easy as building Rome in a day. Will you win every scholarship you apply for?

Definitely not. But if you follow the steps in this book, you won't just secure money to finance your education. You'll also learn new skills, techniques, and ways of looking at things that will serve you well not only during your college and possibly graduate years, but also throughout your life.

The tactics and strategies you employ from this book that help you take full advantage of your scholarship opportunities will be similar to tactics and strategies you'll use throughout college, grad school (if you go for it) and your career. They will enable you to both uncover and maximize every prospect you encounter to move yourself along to the next level.

In today's competitive overcrowded world, we all need to dig a little deeper and work a little harder to stand out from the rest. Remember the lessons this book has taught you and you will achieve what you set out to do.

I did it. And I know you can too.

ABOUT THE AUTHOR

Marvis Burns is a MBA candidate at the Wharton School, University of Pennsylvania where he studies finance and entrepreneurship.

A native of Detroit, MI, Marvis studied business at Cornell University. After winning numerous scholarships and helping his peers win money, Marvis noticed trends. He interviewed many students and organizations to confirm his observations. He is passionate about helpings others, as seen in his endeavors:

Educational Keys, www.educationalkeys.com

Young Leaders for Excellence, www.yl4e.org

Learn more about him at www.marvisburns.com.